LIONTAMING IN AMERICA

Also by Elizabeth Willis

Poetry

Alive: New and Selected Poems
Address
Meteoric Flowers
Turneresque
The Human Abstract
Second Law
Spectral Evidence (with Nancy Bowen)

Essays

Radical Vernacular: Lorine Niedecker and the Poetics of Place
(Editor)

LIONTAMING
IN
AMERICA

Elizabeth Willis

A New Directions Paperbook Original

Manufactured in the United States of America
First published as New Directions Paperbook 1611 in 2024

Library of Congress Cataloging-in-Publication Data
Names: Willis, Elizabeth, author.
Title: Liontaming in America / Elizabeth Willis.
Other titles: Liontaming in America (Compilation)
Description: New York, NY : New Directions Publishing Corporation 2024.
Identifiers: LCCN 2024024837 | ISBN 9780811238632 (trade paperback) | ISBN 9780811238786 (ebook)
Subjects: LCGFT: Poetry.
Classification: LCC PS3573.I456523 L56 2024 |
DDC 811/.54—dc23/eng/20240621
LC record available at https://lccn.loc.gov/2024024837

10 9 8 7 6 5 4 3 2

New Directions Books are published for James Laughlin
by New Directions Publishing Corporation
80 Eighth Avenue, New York 10011

ndbooks.com

CONTENTS

THE END

LOST IN SPACE

SETTLER TIME

THE CINEMA HAS ALWAYS BEEN
INTERESTED IN GOD

BOY

INTERPRETATION OF DREAMS

AND THEN THERE HE WAS,
AS IF EVERYBODY KNEW HIS NAME

THE SNOWS OF YESTERYEAR

MATOAKA & MRS. ROLFE

UNCATEGORICAL FEELINGS

MISS MANNING & MRS. JAMES

PEREGRINATIONS

MISS ADAMS, MRS. COBB & MRS. YOUNG; OR, THE ANGEL OF THE CHURCH AT SALT LAKE; HER ALIEN, HER PROXY

THE ADAMS FAMILY

THE WRITING ON THE WALL

MR. ROBERTS

SOMETIMES

FRIEND & FELLOW WORKER

CLOSE ENCOUNTERS

EARTHWORK

ANYTHING GOES

Begin anywhere

THE END

Finally, my love, I gave in, and it became a now.

It was finally now.

Clarice Lispector, tr. Idra Novey

THE END

This book is not a memoir. Its memories are not mine.

In the making of a poem, there is seldom a traceable path, only a *kind* of genealogy. You follow the leaf to the branch, the branch to the root.

You don't see the dotted line that separates the purple State from the vibrating green Territory. You're in the unlined interior inhabited by names from the world that precedes you, sounds you can't yet pronounce.

Words don't fall onto the page; they rise to meet its hushed expanse.

Routes emerge in retrospect, fixed by repetition. Feet pound out a path through the scrub and grasses, knives of all sizes hacking through the trees. Then one day the line is visible from space.

The Oregon Trail, the Lincoln Highway, the Trail of Tears, the Northwest Passage. Sequence produces neither equivalence nor restitution.

I'm not speaking for you, I'm speaking to you, America.

Your foot still looks for streams and mountain passes, sandbars and natural bridges.

You can't build a highway over every gap you see. You can't make a world by churning out a sidewalk. You don't even know the story you think you're trying to write.

Where, in what shadow of a footprint, did greed start to sound like the whisper of your special god?

A factual sensorium is buried beneath history's serialized fictions. Bodies still floating to the surface, graves erased by chemical lawns, voices thrown downwind.

If you obscure intention, if you hide it in executive edict or legislative will or partisan imperative, you can justify an endless war. If you tuck it in a prophet's cloak, you can call it holy.

Fallible, damaged, contradictory Walt Whitman imagined the nation as a poem. A great poem in need of constant revision. A union of disparate, endlessly modified parts.

The first US states to establish women's suffrage were built on broken treaties and industrialized extraction.

What constitutes a union—and how it touches its constituents—is as variable as the location in which every human stands.

On the high and windy bridge between what can and can't be said, the poem asks a question. How are we going to get across?

The West has been witness to an Idea writing itself with conquest's hand, right to left, East to West, clothed in a rhetoric that claims to be as natural as the planet's turning.

Its pen is not mightier than its sword; it is with a sword that it learned to write.

Such power is both real and imaginary, as the mission of real power is to lay hold upon the imagination.

In most US frontier towns the wooden churches have burned or collapsed; the general store has been leveled to make room for the poured concrete of a supermarket already fallen from its sanitary grandeur into a block of parking spaces; the theaters converted into senior centers or dollar stores or filled with starlings before one agency or another shuts them down.

The Automobile Association of America's guide for Wyoming lists more jails as historical sites than any other category of tourist attraction.

Jails were made to last.

Poetry, the true fiction, was meant to take them down.

Everyone wants to know what happens in the bedroom. What went on before we got here. What we're going to miss later on. How things appeared at the beginning and the end.

Sometimes a man and woman, sometimes a single cell deciding to see the world. Sometimes a grandmother split open to constellate the skies. A turtle, a frog, a bird or seed feeling its way to the sun.

Sometimes a sun, unownable zero, sometimes a void, a breath before the ocean. An arrow, pure inflection, impurely imagined. Edgeless time eating up its dream of space.

The end of a line the first hand takes hold of.

This is how the boat was built. This is how they pulled it ashore. One species or another, followed by a question.

Salvage or slavery, gunpowder or corn, clothing or skin, trees or paragraphs, buffalo or boots, things I haven't thought of.

One book calls it chaos. Another an elaborate order we are too small, too partial, to see in a story subcontracted to the gods.

Another sees the beginning as a tree radiant with unknowing, a being whose future has not yet been written.

The first writer to sign her name to a poem is said to be Enheduanna, a Mesopotamian woman who wrote on a tablet, millennia before Mary's son divided the clock into before and after.

She served Inanna, queen of heaven, who appears with her foot on the back of a lion she's taking on a short-leashed walk.

Part of Inanna's work is domestication. To civilize another creature as a mother would, showing the power of her existence through a body that will outlive her.

Civilization is what makes childhood a captivity narrative.

Writing is a refusal that captivity is the end.

When I was a child, my eye was older than an oak.

From the highest chair, I saw string beans move from my brother's plate into my mother's mouth when my father looked away. I watched my sister spit her peas behind the sink. A dog moved from the woods toward the kitchen door. The house unfolding like a book.

I read my father's secret history of anger, my mother's dissertation on subterfuge, their parlor of doubt, the kitchen of their discontent.

This was my host country and I its virus.

I witnessed a world that couldn't be explained. Rhymed and unrhymed, its alien talk floated above a blanket of verse.

In time, I would adopt its pattern language. I would deliver its messages like a page. I would spy with my little eye. I would open and close like a camera.

In the stories of that planet, I would find no character resembling myself, so I would place myself outside them, in a poem.

When I was a child, I hated lace; I buried all the dolls.

I hid in the snow and thought about what it would mean: to disappear. A little ghost whispering *help!*, testing its alarms.

But when I was grown, I opened the box of broken dolls, and when it was dark, I held the tree by its branches and all the childish words rustled back into the woods, into the purple snow.

I knew there was a story larger than anything.

At the back of the lens, the end was already on fire.

LOST IN SPACE

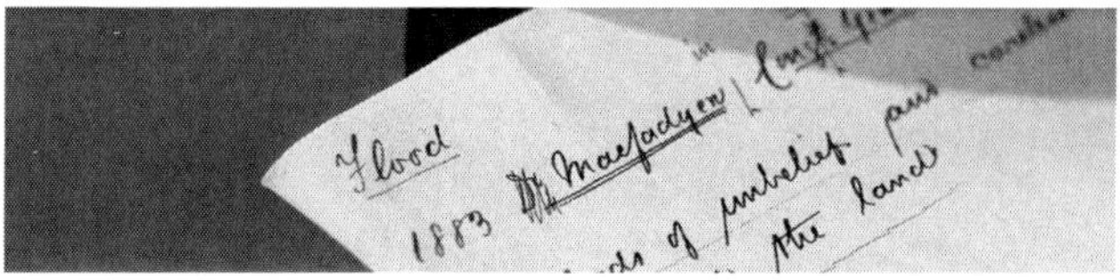
Flood
1883
the land

The line between a father and a madman may be as faint as the breath in a silent letter.

Lots of families have one: the alienated star, the conductor at the lip of the pit, the man with the microphone and the open shirt.

The guy who watches the sky and says it's going to rain.

This one's an ancient little self-made NASA, building a capsule to colonize the next world.

The family, coupled up, ignores the necessity of its own incestuous future. The boat stinks.

Rheumy, thirsty, effluvious. A pail for the food they can't keep down. A pail for the water they hope not to have to drink of. Shit delicately dropped off the edge or covered by the barely edible hay. The stinging air upon every rashy fact.

Factual sex. Factual nakedness. A queasy woolen cloak. Humid, all too humid.

When the boat finds a shore, the father lowers first a chicken, then a goat, then the smallest girl.

And in the mud she plants a seed, and from the seed sprouts a vine. From the vine hangs a grape.

And when the girls have watered and plucked and crushed the grapes born of the seed, and when the boys have bottled what flowed forth and buried it in a hole in the earth, and the darkness of the earth has made it into wine, the unmoored man—the erstwhile prophet, the depressive dictatorial visionary—will drink himself back to sea in the privacy of a tent made of sails.

So it is in the dull aftermath of salvation that when a son arrives at the father's tent to bring him news from the fields, the father is already adrift beyond reach.

He has stupored himself without a coverlet, and his son—yea, his youngest son, whom he has instructed not to touch his own pleasure—has seen him with his hand on the rudder of his own boat.

Aside from the crucifixion of Jesus, Mary's annunciation is the most painted episode in the long, uneven history of narrative painting. But the main event remains invisible. All the artist can do is point at the expensive golden word flying between an adolescent messenger and an adolescent girl who was only looking for a quiet place to read.

It's not uncommon for a girl's youth to be so violently interrupted; for its meaning to be so thoroughly claimed by a future she doesn't own. For history to place her at a threshold guarded by a bunch of men.

When you let an angel into your bedroom, the rest will follow.

A man in a suit will come to your door with a check, you will get a phone call from the bank.

You will smell like the most expensive perfume in the world.

Or two men in suits will arrive with a gift in their hands. One will be handsome, the other slow. They want to be your new best friends, they want you to read their book.

They're asking you to believe in the implausible scene from which their book emerges, just as you might believe without seeing the king of kings crowning in the impossible hole of the mother of God.

Noah's nakedness, like that of other authority figures, is only a
thing because someone saw and someone else spoke of it.

In the drunken vulnerability of power, a ruler may assume its
staffers will drape its embarrassments in bunting, that's what it
means to rule.

Looking will be recast as intrusion. Curiosity as disrespect.

The most important principle in the arts of confidence is that
of diverted attention. Watch my hand carefully. Nothing up the
crazy prophet's sleeve.

When an earthly subject refuses to look away, she is turned into
a column that will dissolve into a heap in the next rain. He is
cursed and made legendary.

Don't look at the angry fire within the bush.

Don't look at the burning city in which your daughters are
offered to strangers by a man trying to appease his terrifying god.

If a family were not placed in a barn or a boat or on an island,
they would carry their story to another world.

They would occupy a stage or be placed in a tiny metal package
and thrown into the sky, where a distant camera would watch
everything they do.

Once the ship sinks or the hatch is locked, they are
extraterritorial. What is their church? What is their state?

The original pilot of *Lost in Space* begins with a shot of the galaxy.

As the camera pans back, we find we are looking not at the
sky but at a screen. It doesn't fill the horizon, just a wall of the
"control center."

The hands at the controls are those of a well-trimmed posse
of uniformed youngsters staring at their blinking consoles or
walking offstage with robotic efficiency.

We think we're watching a drama unfold far out beyond us,
but it's watching us too as we unfold and flower and fall to the
ground.

The date of the action is October 16, 1997. The Future.

In the future, outer space is well funded, and crises are contained
by flashing panels. No one is sweating.

All you have to do is trust the godlike voice of the machine and
the actual existence of the manmade stars.

When an island is too small or cold or its workers are too exhausted to produce everything the family wants, their nation will expand its borders by inventing real estate.

They will take rum and tobacco and land and humans and offer paper or firearms or fabric in trade.

The conquest of space is full of unspoken purposes, just as it was in the War Against Mexico, the War Against Taxes, and the Wars Against Mesopotamia.

The weapons are muskets and lead balls and arrows and smallpox, glass buildings and gasoline, machetes and exploding barrels full of nails. Night goggles, deep-thrust telescopes, hidden cameras.

When the earth is no longer rich enough to fulfill the longings of its richest earthlings, someone who has accrued the most gold and firearms will find a way to send a new A-team into space. There's more than one way to plant a flag.

When the future was 1997, the present was 1965. In Southeast Asia and in space, the US was fighting another Union to colonize a sovereign world that didn't belong to either of them.

In the televised future of the imaginary 1990s, the wealthiest and most educated white subjects project that ten million families a year could be sent to colonize other planets.

But first they need a starter family of handsome chessplayers and mechanics. And an unattached geologist whose sperm will be launched in the direction of their oldest daughter.

Volunteers for the First Family are selected for their "pioneer resourcefulness," for their cheerfulness in the face of uncertainty, for their understanding of physics, and their shiny straight hair.

They are a bunch of Robinsons, a father and mother going to heaven with their kids. The nucleus of a molecule designed to populate outer space.

Dr. Maureen Robinson is wrapped in jiffy-pop foil, bubbly and efficient. Her popcorn breasts fill out the delicate wrapping in a way that suggests an outtake in which the suit is ripped open and something hot and white pops into view.

In order to reach their destination alive, the Robinsons have to hibernate for a century.

The original pilot has been cut and reworked to accommodate a well-meaning robot and the gay-coded, troublemaking Dr. Smith.

A few years into their journey, they are thrown off course. In one version they encounter a meteor belt; in another, Dr. Smith is to blame. The family stays eerily asleep. Their ship crash-lands on a desert planet with breathable Earthlike air.

When they wake up, no one knows if they've gotten far enough to fulfill their plan.

The males go out exploring one of the planet's mountains. They see a footprint, then a shaggy cyclops who traps the smooth-skinned men in a cave until their smaller, smoother-skinned replica pierces the creature's heart with his spacegun.

But the first action on the planet is June Lockhart playing Dr. Maureen Robinson doing the laundry and preparing dinner under a makeshift tent with the help of her daughters and other domestic appliances.

Women carry things and prepare. They "hold down the fort."

In the religion of recruitment, it's no longer possible to distinguish between soldiers and children, women and machines.

The children live in an allegory: they're there to clarify the stakes of empire. The intrepid Will and the shiny Penny are linked to a story so large they cannot outrun it.

Penelope will wait a long time to marry an alien, or a brother, or a brother-in-law.

Will will always be fighting to enter the company of men. If he cannot have his father, he will join Dr. Smith. This thought is a source of horror to Mr. and Mrs. Robinson. They would rather he bond with a machine.

Late in the *Lost in Space* pilot, when they're on the run from climate change, the Robinsons arrive at the shore of a vast lake.

The van they're driving suddenly has to swim. They're tossed around like crazy, lightning all around them.

They're being batted back and forth between Greek mythology, the Bible, and the origins of the novel.

The world doesn't move two by two into and out of their little ark. There are queer figures who disrupt the symmetry, who threaten the enabling family narrative.

When the storm has passed and they wash up on a beach, they're suddenly in a Garden, tempted by alien fruits, aware of their inappropriate clothes.

Because they believe they're alone, they're in a state of grateful wonder, unashamed.

Led by Mr. Robinson, they kneel in their first prayer.

Our vantage point is that of the snake, the alien, the native. We can see in the colonists what they cannot see of themselves.

That they haven't found their place; they have only become more lost.

When Robinson Crusoe got into a boat, he didn't bring his wife and children, or his sheep and goats or laundry basket. He was only a boy who disobeyed his parents.

When he left home, the ship he joined was probably a slaving vessel.

Off the coast of Africa, the ship sank, and the boy was enslaved by a Moorish pirate, who kept him for two years on the coast of a many-peopled continent. When he escaped from bondage, his first project was to capture a boy of his own.

His *misfortunes,* as he called them, didn't cure *his passion for the sea.* Eventually he sailed again, and when he shipwrecked on an island, he fell apart and remade himself.

Saved by the book that washed up from the wreck, Crusoe began to think about Adam.

He was a lonely subject until he became a protagonist who only needed one name.

Everything happened in episodes because only so much could be thought at once.

The shipwrecked man creates a monarchy of one.

When he sees a footprint, he panics.

He has to keep writing, so he has to build a table, for which he has to make a chair.

He must find dry powder. He wants a fence.

He thinks more than ever about the scent of roasting meat.

He thinks about the coins in his pockets. Just a bunch of heads.

He thinks of his book's previous authors.

A handful of shells needs another person to establish the magical qualities of exchange, to build the fence that will turn the wilderness into a garden and the garden into a plantation.

He will melt the coins to forge the tracks to move his story along.

He can't explain why he thinks that all his book's words—the preface, the conclusion, the acknowledgments, and all the chapters in between—belong to him.

Does the sensation of authorship explain his desire to hold reality together by killing whatever doesn't build him a bridge to the next episode?

Or vice versa. Did killing turn him into an author?

Whatever he leaves unwritten, whatever he doesn't have the words for, will not exist.

He calls this a history, as if its perspective were everyone's.

As if he were writing everybody's autobiography, a book before its time.

He encounters another man whose status he endlessly tries to clarify.

Anything he doesn't kill becomes part of his economy.

Everything beyond his wordy mind becomes an object that can be taken or cast away.

Robinson Crusoe's author was a dissenter, an outlaw, and a debtor, the writer of a banned book and a secret agent for the king. The warrant for his arrest described him as *a middle-sized, spare man, about forty years old, of a brown complexion, and dark brown hair, but wears a wig.*

Mr. Defoe survived the Great Plague of 1665, the Great Fire of 1666, and the Great Storm of 1703. His mother died when he was nine or ten. He was imprisoned at Newgate, and still changed the careening path of English literature.

He invented a form that would be reproduced millions of times: in *Tarzan*, in *I Love Lucy*, in *The Munsters*.

Historically speaking, the *Swiss Family Robinson* (1812) bridges the centuries between *Robinson Crusoe* and *Lost in Space*: its story was invented by a Swiss minister who wanted to teach family values to his sons without having to talk about sex.

The problem of *encounter* between, for instance, the alien and the native or between the monstrous and the beautiful is reiterated and mediated by the contested authority of narrative.

Each iteration hinges on a conversation with difference. You're folded back into the family or spat out into the dark.

A stranded family, like a royal family, demonstrates the way a system of complicity can be mass produced. This is their primary labor on the set.

Complicity, their story says, is the cost of belonging.

SETTLER TIME

THE GREATEST
Natural & National
CURIOSITY
IN THE WORLD.

In the beginning: words. Anatomy. Anger. Astonishment.

Apple. Boxelder. Circumstance.

Animal husbandry. Murder. Corn.

A well, a shovel.

The end belonged to syntax. She did. He did. Eat. Partake of. Something. Forbidden. He was. They were. Captured. Cast out. He was. We were. Unburied. Lifting Off.

In between was the play within the play, nouns weighing their actions, complicating, conjugating, repeating.

In between was the idea of beginnings and endings. Paperwork.

In between was where the story of everything out of sight took shape, swerved.

The crisis of 1620. The disaster of 1692. King William's War. Queen Anne's War. King George's War. The War of Jenkins' Ear.

Every action had a wage, was a wager. Silver and copper drew their lines upon the region between the fire and the clouds. Pine tree money, lion dollars, pieces of eight conducting their bright quadrille across the unsteady backdrop of a map.

Territories were flagged, ruched, stitched open.

The panic of 1819. The panic of 1837. The panic of 1873.

States were states of mind having an argument in black and white and playing it out, like a game that becomes a war, upon the fields.

The rising action climbed the curved horizon of a hill. The story and the landscape, the metaphor and the plot.

A hunger for endlessness puts the story on repeat.

Suddenly every body is assigned a proxy life in miniature among the tin soldiers and fences and model forts or in the shifting grounds of the woods or among the open wilds of native grass.

Here they must anticipate carefully their relation to what comes next. Consider the silent contracts of the gift.

Only heaven appears in Technicolor. Only heaven claims to read the map from above.

Treaties. Typhoid. Whooping cough.

Only an alien language would believe it could have the last word.

Zealot. Zenith. Zion.

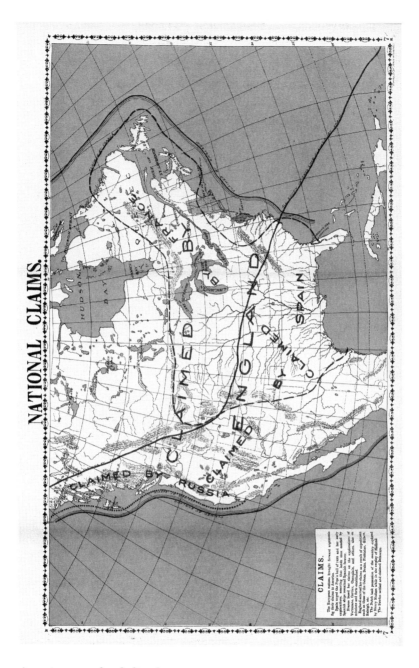

NATIONAL CLAIMS.

A region may be defined

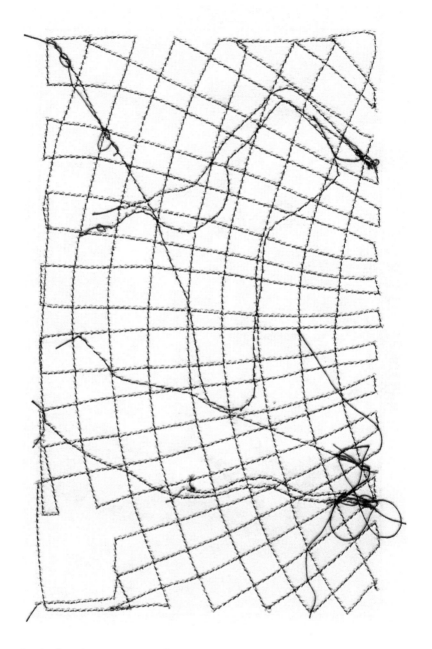

by its barriers to perception.

The word comes to shore from the Middle French. A *pionnier* was a laborer employed in digging.

In English it was a member of the infantry who went ahead of its regiment to prepare the ground: digging trenches, repairing roads, clearing scrub. In obsolete usage, it meant a sapper or underminer, the one who dug up mines when a troop was under siege.

It meant a miner, a quarrier. A laborer or porter.

In the colonial record regarding the Cochinaug land seized by Europeans in the 17th century, a document full of cheating and punishment, it was ruled that soldiers who had lost their weapons in wagers of cards or dice or as a result of other sins or negligence would be designated *pioneers* or scavengers until they were able to re-arm themselves.

Francis Bacon delineated two categories of natural philosophers: *some to bee Pionners, and some Smythes.*

Some dig; others forge.

Some prepare; others make.

Undermining, taking away one thing in order to clear the way for something else, is in one instance a form of punishment and in another an occasion for high praise.

In his *Letters from an American Farmer*, Hector St. John de Crèvecoeur wrote of European pioneers in America as precursors and outcasts, earnest and ingenious authors of otherwise unwritten histories, improvers of previously uncultivated lands.

When he referred to their "progress" he meant their forward movement into the interior, not their success after they got there.

In Crèvecoeur's fictive epistles, agrarian colonists are portrayed as agents of a gently civilizing and domesticating force in opposition to the hunting culture of the continent's native peoples.

Is he ignorant of North America's long history of cultivation by its first peoples and their horticultural survival training of invasive Europeans a century before his arrival, or does he prefer to forget it?

After emigrating to New France as a young man, Crèvecoeur settled in the section of the New York colony then designated as Orange County, after the Prince of Orange, who would later become King William III of England and Ireland, William II of Scotland, and husband of his cousin Mary, the daughter of the beheaded Charles I.

What was Crèvecoeur seeing and not seeing amid all that regal newness?

Even some of his contemporaries had figured out that this land, like the old one, had existed for millions of years, and that its appearance was constantly in flux, though there is little evidence that he or any of his friends had a sense of the sophistication of the American civilizations that predated them.

What was new to Crèvecoeur was entirely familiar to the Munsee people, who had grown and preserved a variety of crops and shared them with the peculiarly pink-skinned strangers who embarrassed themselves with their strutting down their wide-ruled fields.

The newness of New England and New York and New France and New London, its linking of space to time, its division into past and future, was an adaptation of the rhetoric of good and evil that served the gamblers, opportunists, zealots, and refugees who were seeking to shake off the old.

When someone to whom the land was new saw the light, when they were converted, when they were beginning again, they began to believe *they* were new.

They could see themselves at the beginning of a timeline on which anything seemed possible.

Asking what is old and what is new, what is native and what is invasive is one step into historical self-knowledge.

Where does this begin? Where do I end? Where does the story lead? On what ground do our bodies meet?

Some of the people whose genetic ladders prop up the cells of my primary organs were pioneers. A few may have been card players, but mostly they were diggers and railroad workers, weavers, and seamstresses.

One rode by horseback to assist other women with the bloody mess of birth. One buried the ones who didn't make it.

One leaned permanently forward, creased by the belt she'd been given to pull a tub of coal through spaces too narrow for a mule.

Some wrote accounts of their lives in obedience to a system that structured their thinking and had a stake in which stories they told.

Their language was not forbidden.

Some were murdered, a few accused of witchcraft, crushed to death by the obscure logic of their time and place.

They were not, according to their own histories, violent people. Neither well-schooled nor wholly ignorant.

From the disordered heap they left behind, they appear to have been more pragmatic than self-righteous.

I've found no record of their thoughts about the effect of their presence on the land where they squatted, nor their effect on the health of the people who belong to the land from which they drew water for their plum trees and corn.

When they outlasted a bad winter, they called themselves blessed. When the baby who died of measles didn't kill everyone else.

When they paused at a location whose name they didn't know,

sometimes they called it by a place they once had lived. Lanark, Aberdeen. Or dreamed of. Paris. Jerusalem. Or an allegorical backdrop they could only imagine. Bountiful.

Some came to rest in the slim shadow of their privilege.

Some fed soldiers heading into one war or another, part of a system so vast it was hard to locate. But sometimes they seemed to have a feeling.

When a stranger who borrowed a pony brought it back just in time for it to die. When they were cheated out of a bag of grain by someone who had more than they did. When it got personal.

The sun wheeled west, and they didn't seem to consider turning another way. That was how their story went.

It's not easy for a pioneer to see the hole he's digging because he's standing in it.

The vulnerability of the figurehead is at the center of Jean-Michel Basquiat's painting of Charles I: most kings get their heads cut off.

When English dissenters put the concept of divine right on trial in 1649, it was Charles I's head that rolled into the London gutter. Neither God nor Milton would save him.

His judges and executioners fled, or tried to flee, to the semi-theocratic world of the Connecticut colony to hide among other puritans and *pionniers*.

Everything is torqued by the syntax of relation: a supreme subject becomes an object, who once made objects of his subjects.

When the tables of power turned over on the historical King, and later turned on his judges and executioners, bodies were exhumed, dismembered, their heads put on spikes for public display, their pieces thrown into a mass grave.

The image of the colonies is a snake chopped into thirteen slices.

The image of the president is a slaveholder cutting down a tree.

Regicide and fugitivity, crime and escape from punishment.

Exile Anne Hutchinson; publish Cotton Mather. Elect Thomas Jefferson; deny Sally Hemings. Empower Clarence Thomas; pillory Anita Hill.

Watch the house of social death being built for anyone who tells.

When a preacher wants to show you what's behind his curtain, look at what he's doing with his other hand.

Something more valuable will always be held back. A weapon held in tension between real and symbolic power. Between personal and systemic deeds.

Within his 1822 self-portrait, Mr. Charles Willson Peale pulls aside a velvet drape to reveal a caged menagerie and gallery, more laboratory than studio.

He is not the only colonial to gut and stuff the world to make its beauty last beyond what his unregulated power wants to do with it.

A century later, in *Parson Weems' Fable*, Grant Wood combines the shrugging hospitality of Peale with a classic portrait of Washington.

Parson Weems was the entrepreneurial preacher who invented the myth of presidential truthfulness to fuel sales of his biography of Washington's imaginary youth. Mr. Peale is his contemporary, a master of trompe l'oeil who rode beside him on the coattails of national power.

Both paintings toy with the pretense of revelation held open by its human figures. But only the later one directs our attention to the complicity of naturalist violence and nationalist fiction.

In 1939, Mr. Wood is tired. He needs to talk about this double deception. He's been living publicly while stuck in a closet. His life's a mess.

Even his cherry trees are fringed like a curtain; the brown-skinned workers gathering fruit in the background are probably enslaved.

We move within the fictions of cheerful servitude and boyish innocence. The bodies posed so correctly, they pry at the disclosure of a reality beyond artifice.

Everything eventually points into the shadow of a national lie.

The first circus in the barely united States pitched its tent in Philadelphia in 1793. Its equestrian theater caught the attention of a Washington still unused to riding on the other side of insurrection.

The event's potential for nation-building would later re-emerge in the white nostalgia of Buffalo Bill's Great Wild West Show, which merged scenes of racial conflict with other fictions of prowess, captivity, and liberation. A passion play of colonial life and death to redistribute the racial imaginaries of disunited territories.

If you are standing on a horse, you want to move in a circle as fast as possible, to turn the ring into a centrifuge that will keep your feet in place.

Mr. Charles Willson Peale had painted the president leaning on a chair or a cannon, with little men on horseback in the coppery distance, but at the back of his eye the former general was already hypnotized by a vision of his future on a bright horse cast in bronze with all the little men looking on.

What moves in a straight line eventually disappears. What moves in a circle can live forever.

By the early nineteenth century, circuses were less equestrian and more like traveling, semi-educational zoos.

It wasn't until mid-century that they shifted their attention to liontamers and other demonstrations of power that conflated "natural" and national hierarchies defined by race, gender, or species.

Here we pause while the set rotates behind the curtain.

Behold P. T. Barnum in his Connecticut home, a white man in his early twenties determined to reinvent the US circus as a museum of anomalies.

Joice Heth, now in her 80s, has been sold to this man, who will exhibit her as the 161-year-old wet nurse of George Washington.

When she dies less than a year later, he arranges a public autopsy for which he charges fifty cents admission.

Between the stanzas of the national epic you can see the seams that hold its images together.

Is that a spider web in the background of the dollar bill or what.

A razorwire fishing net, a green-backed border wall.

What lives within the container of your skin.

On which side of the equation do you feel the weight of an unpayable debt.

The History Channel refers to Buffalo Bill and Sitting Bull as *strange friends*, deviating, that is, from the stories that placed them in staged and real opposition.

In William Notman's 1885 studio photograph, they stand before a lightly wooded backdrop on a rug of simulated prairie grass.

Mr. Cody's body—his Van Dyke and thigh-high boots, embroidered shirt and moleskin pants cinched with a large buckle—is torqued so he can point in two directions at once.

He leans toward Sitting Bull as his eyes and hands point away, his right elbow braced against his companion's left arm, his hand fixed in an upward diagonal.

He looks like he's trying to show Sitting Bull where to go while signaling something bigger about a future he doesn't think his co-star can see.

The composition suggests that the indigenous boredom of one man is holding the energetic white explorer back.

Each has a hand on the rifle that bisects the space between them. Cody's is higher, but it is his *strange friend* whose hand can reach the trigger.

Sitting Bull's face says it's not him but this dandy who is caught in the phantastic glare of the past, a world that can't tell the difference between deception and magic, conquest and survival.

His gaze seems to land on the pale hand emerging from Cody's unwrinkled shirt. This man has so little to offer him.

They're at a tipping point between performance and refusal.

In the distance you can see the company behind Cody's well-groomed horse racing in a straight line into the dust cloud of its own collapse.

When viewed from the horsehair seat of a railroad car, the land over which a creature flies may appear to spool out like a motion picture, each frame approaching the eye at a pace as yet undreamed, so breathtaking it feels more like letting go than taking in.

From a distance, the presumed passenger of such a carriage, this hypothetical audience of the continental interior, may reveal no sensation of driving the narrative they inhabit; but, rather, having purchased the temporary dwelling of their seat and parted clouds of dust and crickets, they may be as pleased with their own endurance of a world beyond their command as they are awed by a technology that surpasses common understanding.

The carriage (subject) carries them (object). This is what occurs to one.

Here are the latecomers of means and the servants they brought with them who sat on wooden benches, farther back.

The hotel-owners and politicians and doctors and European tourists who encountered the continental West by train had many origins, which they rewrote over and over. They legislated; they reviewed.

They changed the wording of a text or the location of the line, or they changed the meaning of the words so that they always arrived at the beginning, with a great expanse ahead.

He who was carried by the passive voice, she without property, moving mechanically into a climactic complicity of fates, as when two forces are in motion, one may appear to be joining something rather than breaking it apart.

THE CINEMA HAS ALWAYS BEEN INTERESTED IN GOD

A man walks into a bar.

He's looking for a pack of smokes, and in the screen-set suburbs of Hollywood, that's the nearest place to find them. His wife wears a housecoat in the kitchen snapping beans, folding napkins.

Here's the plan.

If you want to smoke, you go to the bar. If you want to be alone, you close the swinging door to the kitchen. If you want to buy a bike, you get a paper route.

The trees have just been planted. The lawn needs to be watered. Your house doesn't have any spare rooms. If you have extra time, you spend it in the garage or in the yard.

Rain is upsetting.

Weekends are upsetting. They involve a buddy being late for bowling, or an in-law visiting your wife, or your child going missing, or taking on additional chores, or closing the kitchen door.

If you need to be alone and your wife is already in the kitchen, you walk to the nearest lounge, saying you're going to buy a pack of smokes.

You can't escape the soundstage.

Cigarettes are sold, like dress shirts, by clean-cut actors who believe in the "T-zone." You buy them, you bring them home.

This is Joe and Mary, a classic Christian team. They're losing their footing among the little ways of Babylon, they're "just like us."

She's pregnant and long suffering, falling in the kitchen.

He's angry at the car, which doesn't start, and at the cop who rides a motorcycle all day in the sun, taking notes on his speed and his style of driving.

Joe Smith puts each ticket in his mouth as if he were being asked to eat his own actions, to swallow the law, to submit to anything this skinny cop in leather boots might think of inflicting on a straight guy whose ride needs a new starter and who has to eat his cornflakes before he takes his boy to school on his way to the job for which he will always be late.

The term "military industrial complex" has not yet been spoken. Ronald Reagan does not yet mean an airport or a governor, just an actor who sells cigarettes, whose father was a union man and a drinker with the Santa Ana dust on his mouth.

When Mr. Smith speaks, he seems almost to be barking.

When the boy and the father argue, it's the mom who "takes a beating."

When God speaks on the radio, Mr. Smith says "Let's just see how great his miracles really are."

Mrs. Smith has a secret off-screen past in which her other name is Nancy. She's dating a young actor she has not yet told she is pregnant.

When her husband in the movie is about to carve the Sunday roast, she gasps with a pain in her tented belly.

At the hospital, a cartoon stork says, "I've never lost a father yet." This is the language of an empty twilit room in which men think what have they done? What will they do?

Wheeled out of surgery on a metal cart, Mary flickers like a corpse. She's breathing in the antiseptic air. She has no other words to say.

In a crowded church across town, a preacher speaks about men and women and children of every race, station, and color, but when the camera pans the room, everyone it sees is white.

"Everyone" is cautiously hopeful.

On TV we are watching Nancy, an actress, become less like Mary while her boyfriend becomes less like his father.

In a few years, this town will be the set of an invasion of alien communist ants.

In the faces of Mary and Joseph, we see Nancy believing in the star system, we see Ronnie believing in Nancy.

We see the sun in the heavens. We see God overhead like a great idea at the blinding center of the bulb.

Sometime after performing an archetypal pregnancy with an ordinary Joe, Miss Nancy Davis will marry the witch-hunting director of the Screen Actor's Guild.

As governor of California, Mr. Reagan will support women's reproductive rights, but when he moves up, he'll perform the role of anti-choice candidate for the evangelical right.

Miss Davis will become the front person of the "Just Say No" campaign, a billboard that obscures more than it reveals.

Who tips the scales. Who wipes down the weapon. Who's going to cover for the man behind the cardboard wall.

A man walks into an aircraft assembly plant. The sound he hears in the distance is a sentence about World War II, which has not yet been translated.

Today it sounds like a job. It smells like store-bought clothes.

All the men hammer against this theme music. Busy, random phrases warming up for their entry into a symphonic structure.

Everyone is listening. Everyone believes in the machine. Everyone wants to have more butter than they used to.

In the hangar-sized studio just behind the credits, Robert Young is surrounded by targets. He has entered a collage, the composition of a century.

On the assembly floor, he becomes this other piece of work, a ghostly interior clothed in the showmanship of working-class skepticism and desire. His name is Joe.

Are the targets painted on the Vultee P-66 Vanguard fighters—on the bottom of the wing and on the back of the fuselage—a tease to the other side? A decoy?

Somewhere across the humming southern swath of the continent, Jasper Johns is drawing circles on a cottony piece of construction paper. He is twelve years old.

A messenger pulls Joe from the floor.

He's headed to the big round sink crowned with borax dispensers. In the background a poster shows the influence of Russian Futurism.

Its words form an emphatic diagonal toward an enormous gray ear. *The only person interested in your opinions is the enemy.*

In the factory's expensive executive office Mr. Smith is asked: Do you go to church? Do you believe in God? Do you have children?

How much money do you have in the bank?

When Joe refuses to say how much money he has saved, he gets the nod.

The nod has been traveling from Washington to LA in search of people who like to keep secrets. Joe will be working in a special tent, placing special bombs into special airplanes.

From now on everything he touches will be privileged. His job is to balance all this privilege on the thinnest wire between good and evil.

*

When Joe drives his kid to school, he stays to watch him join the other kids around a flagpole. The California sun has turned the lawn into a stage. The theme of the day is Nathan Hale. Give me liberty or give me death.

When everyone pledges allegiance, they don't say *under God*. They don't reveal the contents of their bank accounts.

When they pledge allegiance, they don't put their hands over their hearts, they stretch their arms out diagonally above their heads.

Joe's face is framed in the darkened car window. He is not yet a well-paid TV doctor. The movement of all these white arms doesn't alarm him. Nothing rhymes with anything yet.

Joe can draw a blueprint of a plane from memory. Joe knows where a bomb will be dropped on the grid of a continent viewed from the air.

When he leaves his special tent inside the aircraft assembly plant and starts to drive home, he's followed by a car that is faster and more expensive than his own.

When he speeds up, it speeds up. When he turns suddenly, it turns suddenly. When it runs his car off the road, men in suits jump out to meet him.

When men in suits don't meet you in an executive office but run you off the road, you feel yourself rhyme with a man on a scaffold.

You're Nathan Hale. You'll be blindfolded, and you'll stare at the shoes of your captors. You won't think of anything appropriate to say. You'll just take the punches.

The kind of men who wear suits and drag you to an empty house wear fancy shoes, but they are not properly polished.

They wear expensive things that they would rather throw away than take care of. They play cards beneath a bare bulb. They are immigrants like Nathan Hale, finding their way up a different set of stairs.

When Nathan Hale seems to be knocked unconscious, he is dragged down the stairs, put into the expensive car, driven across Los Angeles County, and dumped on the side of the road.

Joe remembers everything he heard when he was Nathan Hale. He writes symbols on the sidewalk that will help the police retrace the movement of the expensive car back to the house.

Like Odysseus, he'll be a hero because he pays attention, because he can tell a story.

In the end, Joe will manage to get home, where he will finally get to eat at the polished dining room table reserved for special company.

His story will be shaken silly. It will be repeated again and again. It will be beaten to death.

In an ancient book there was a man who lived on location in the desert. At noon he wrestled with the sun the way Jacob wrestled with a hot human angel all night long.

When he got up from the dust, he had a new name that rhymed with his old one. Paul was the exemplary convert.

On film it's Pauline who's in the wilderness—a confused ideal of vulnerability and strength, of genius and foolish luck.

The perils of her serialized life unfold among other encounters with identity staged on nearby sets.

Oscar Apfel and Cecil B. DeMille are codirecting what is said to be the first full-length feature whose centerpiece is not Pauline's starched curls upon the rails, but a frontier pileup of cultural, sexual, and class anxiety in the interracial West.

Conquest and ruin are the stars of a new experience of time and inevitability.

The clock is the god of film. Speed it up. Run it in reverse.

Take the body in your arms. Before you reach the falls.

BOY

A poet's room is a boy's room.

George Oppen

In the 1820s and '30s western New York was said to be scorched with the religious fervor of a great awakening.

Some of the awakened were veterans of the revolution, boys and men who had killed and pioneered for a barely united snake that had no gold to pay them. Their compensation was to take the form of land grants.

But first they had to perform the disappearance of the villages and people of the Haudenosaunee nation, a task taken on by the Sullivan Campaign's bloody team spirit in the 1790s.

Campaign is the most common euphemism for what unspeakably happened. A scorched earth policy is exactly what it sounds like.

The story the campaigners told was that the Iroquois were traitors because they sided with the British.

But it was the British with whom the Haudenosaunee had made peace, and they had chosen to honor their agreements rather than side with insurrectionists who had already shown a lack of respect for their elders and for the performative magic of their own words.

Those who claimed the land in payment for military services built settlements reanointed with an ancient past that directed attention away from their crimes: western civilization transferred like a blanket of stones. Rome. Syracuse. Ithaca. Naples. Troy.

It sounded like a sojourn through the ancient world rather than the spoils of attempted genocide.

After the war and before the digging of the Erie Canal, someone decided that the native people who survived Sullivan's rampage would be offered cotton, wool, and chintz, by-products of the slave trade, in return for unspecified US transit and trade rights.

If you travel on the Eisenhower Highway between Seneca Falls, home of Harriet Tubman and of the women's rights convention; Palmyra, birthplace of Mormonism; and Rochester, home of Frederick Douglass and Eastman Kodak, you will pay a toll to the state of New York which sends annually to the Haudenosaunee Confederacy a symbolic shipment of cloth.

A boy walks into the woods. A montage of first-growth and punk shoots skipping off a low cluster of homesteads.

The air tinged with iron and sawdust. His coat too broad, not long enough.

Itching, conjectural, not from around here. Walking off the farm, digging one hole after another.

A beaded light threads the jagged beech, the ash, the sycamore.

The slant of four o'clock: particulate, precise. The formal feeling of an appointment. Traces of a native path in the dark beyond his feet.

The boy is stitched into this world by all the glare behind it. He's been pierced through the eye, through the ear, his body pulled by invisible strings.

A village in the upstate area of Tolland has been renamed Palmyra after a ruined Syrian city. It has banished the Iroquois and welcomed the King of France.

Its men are plowing among the pre-Columbian mounds.

Some believe they've been saved to perform a new part. Outside the crackle of the revival tent, a roaring silence.

The world is a sound the boy no longer recognizes. He wants to make it speak a language he understands.

Above the leaf rot, he sees transparent figures hovering in pillars and streaming curtains.

The boy walks into this lacy wall, his movements an overture to a larger production.

Everything in the big green room pushes forward, thinking of the sun.

Or it bounces like a whistle while the light falls in between, as if its gods intended nothing but this counterpoint of round and sharp and solid lucency.

When someone is coming in a straight line to knock your words out of you and replace them, one by one, with his, you'll feel a change in the air just before it happens.

When he falls, the boy will locate himself at the center of a sound, he will pin himself to an imaginary grid made of time.

He will try to name his position as precisely as possible: "last" or lost" or "later" or "latter."

Treasure hunter, troublemaker, gold-digger. That's him stumbling off the gravelly farm.

But when the light threads his pockets, when it falls on him in a straight line, the trouble is only starting, the gun is being reloaded, the treasure placed upon a cushion in his mind then taken by a long golden arm back into the dirt.

The fields are full of stones. The forest has not yet been pulped.

The canal connecting New York City to Buffalo has not yet passed the print shop.

Everything his father owns is worth nothing. He's indebted to the whole world.

God is becoming king of western New York. He's shaking up the sky and pulling everything toward him like a sun to the west.

He doesn't fall; he descends. He travels in a straight line, very fast.

He wants to know everything about you.

How much money do you have in the bank, Joe?

Do you go to church?

They live in a cabin before moving to a saltbox.

They're coopers and farmers, not as pious as you'd think. Friendly enough with their neighbors that the Durfees bail them out when they almost lose the farm.

They're digging for gold or for water. They have or have not been swindled by a sea captain.

Their boy says he gets his truth from a messenger who floats above the floor. This is the story that takes his family from the dark into a new relation with the public and the law.

They're beginning to live in a future whose past one of them has just begun to write.

See this then

The boy's desire
to belong

Middle child
Mama's song

Witching boy who
hears the ground speak

Boy of the thundering
slot-machine god

Boy who believes
only women can save him

When the music ended, the boy would wander. Upstairs, around town.

Insulted by fences; in love, like Augustine, with the fruit on the other side.

Even Genesis made bodies out of chaos, human and non-human shifting in the wings, creatures rising from the same mud as a tree.

The boy's new religion would re-enact a story of nakedness and leaves, fruit and temptation, larceny and exile.

A snake can make you see a piece of fruit without forgetting the snake is there. This is one form of double vision.

How would the motion of the boy's hand be read by the man behind the curtain or the two-way mirror.

From here on out, he'll keep an eye on you just as he feels himself being watched.

None of this was written down.

It is unclear, or rather there are divergent accounts of, when the boy was done with boyhood or what the end of boyhood was.

At the time, rumors of buried treasure bounced through the burned-over counties of New York and Pennsylvania, building up a furious quest for diggers.

Some were said to be gifted in locating riches that seemed to be waiting for them underground.

In this way any piece of earth could be the site in which a new or an old world was discovered, and a boy could plug into its current with whatever desires were in the air.

When he hired out for digging in rural Pennsylvania, young Mr. Smith encountered a Miss Emma Hale, whose household he soon thereafter joined.

He never, in short, quite had an adulthood without women.

What did he say? Was the promise between them specific or general, public or secret?

Here I put my ear to the ground. Here I light the fire and ask them to come.

Now comes the part with visionary swoons beneath the straight hand of noon.

It was said the boy had stopped his labors in the orchard, faint from the discourse of angels through the night.

In the hill was a story imprinted on sheets of gold.

This was the book he either wrote or copied or translated from leaves only a few witnesses could touch.

It was said he had to look away to see the words. Into a hat, into the stones, into the dark.

Think of Narcissus and of Morrissey gazing into their glassy pools.

The book's first edition lists the young Smith as "AUTHOR AND PROPRIETOR."

He said he was writing the story of the people to whom the hills belonged.

When a body asks a question, meanings may flow wildly through its arms and be taken down as words.

This is where I sit in the doomed arc of evening to tell you about my day.

One November morning, when I'm living near the tip of a long, glaciated finger of New York's Seneca Lake, I drive further north and west to buy an indoor bike from the classifieds.

The road to Egypt, Macedon, and Palmyra takes me past Ganondagon, a thriving information center on the site of what used to be a thriving Haudenosaunee village, where I learn what a yard of wool was once worth in trade for nails or knives.

This is the place whose destruction the first president of the union of states ordered in his first term. Since then, I am told, all presidents of the alien union inhabit a word that in the Haudenosaunee language means approximately "city-destroyer."

At the time of the first city-destroyer, the Haudenosaunee had built a peaceful democracy and six-nation alliance often referred to as the Iroquois Confederacy.

The least obvious difference between this democracy and that of the alien union was that Haudenosaunee women held, among other things, the right to vote.

Eventually this gave nearby settlers like Mrs. Matilda Joslyn Gage and Mrs. Elizabeth Cady Stanton some ideas about what women like themselves might demand.

On the backroads shaped by property lines: the flags of city-destroyers among cardboard signs arguing against the rights of native sovereignty.

I'm following the directions of someone named Blake, who meets me by a garage next to a parking lot attached to a funeral home which he previously called a "business location." I try out his bike in the sudden northern wind, pedaling toward a white hearse without going anywhere at all.

Going home, I will pass the woods where the boy saw gods in the light among the trees.

This is the epicenter of the religion I landed in because my mother's mother's mother's mother had a dream about the boy and joined his story more than a century before my feet touched earth.

The visitor's center resembles the kind of renovated rest area that simulates the shape but not the scale of an early New England home.

I'm told the Smiths came to Palmyra for the inexpensive farmland; no one mentions the father's love of drink or his ill-fated attempts at upward mobility.

The Sister who invites me in believes the Erie Canal is part of a divine plan.

Beyond the log cabin replica with perfect curtains pulled to the side and Lincoln Log corners, I meet a woman who says she saw the shadow of the prophet on an informational placard.

In the piercing light, I see no image of a man, just jagged wounds in a tree where someone has written their family name.

Here he made a book to shore up a church.

By the waters of Babylon. On the Seneca banks.

It was decided in a borrowed room just past the farm of a Mr. Rose of Virginia whose slave quarters they would walk past on the way to their first dunk.

This was the country someone else would call a poem.

Barbaric vast and wild.

Here is the steeple. A faith farm, a gamble, a house of. One world flooding in to touch another.

Its hands are on your shoulders, in your pockets, on your head, touching everything you were.

In your hair, a downdraft. In the chimney, in the throat.

A word comes out of its mouth into yours.

The church is an analogy built to beam the heavens down to you, to open your purselike heart to the heavens.

How do you get in. How do you get out.

Its hands are real hands. You feel its fingerprints. Its ink is writing a different story against your skin. It has your number. It knows your address.

Now you belong to it like a page to a book.

INTERPRETATION OF DREAMS

The poverty of my dreams mortifies me.

Charles Lamb

She is turning
to a meadow
of peculiar pleasantness
in which stand two trees
of great height, she
interprets them afterward
as representations of
her husband and
his brother Jesse
but what she sees
there are trees
very beautiful and well
proportioned where
their branches gloriously
spread themselves

One is surrounded
with a bright belt
and when a breeze passes
the tree is encircled
with goldenness and more
animated as it seems
to express its own joy
and the stream that runs
beneath the tree
shares all the tree's
sensations, swelling
and receding
in response until
both are exceeding
glorious

he is decrepit and alone
traveling on a desolate
road or in a gloomy desert
a desert without sun
in a death-like silence
this was repeated at least
seven times Lucy
called them visions
this was the boy's
father on the subject
of his sojourns

wherein one
exceeding white
and brilliant
was had by one
called destitute
of genius

for he saw what
he saw the man's
naked hands
and ankles
his head and neck
and he had no
other clothing

but this whiteness
his robe
being open
was true
it being glorious
beyond description
like lightning

Belief relies on absence. All else is knowledge.

If seeing is believing, touching is knowing.

A resurrected god returns to his disciples wearing the same body he left behind so they can feel his wounds.

The presence of a witness brings events into language.

After that, language itself is the event.

AND THEN THERE HE WAS,
AS IF EVERYBODY KNEW HIS NAME

*We are all a little wild here with numberless projects
of social reform.*

Ralph Waldo Emerson to Thomas Carlyle

Angel
Apostle
Banker
Beloved
Boss
Brother
Chieftain
Deceiver
Despot
Elder
False Prophet
General
Holy Joe
Indian lover
Infidel
Libertine
Mahomet
Mayor
Mountebank
Mystifier
Novelist
Pope
President
Profiteer
Prophesier
Restorator
Revelator
Secretary
Seer
Slave lover
Thief
Traitor
Translator
Treasure seeker
Tyrant
Wrestler

Surnames are family names and so in the history of the individual it is of no importance what the family name is or has been. Angell. Adams. Smith. Snow. Young.

Anna Nicole Smith
Bessie Smith
Bubba Smith
Burl "Gopher" Smith
Caleb Blood Smith
Cordwainer Smith
Dallas Smith
Delia Smith
Dodie Smith
The Honorable Elias Smith
Emmitt Smith
George J. ("Germany") Smith
Giles Alexander Smith
Jaclyn Smith
Jessie Wilcox Smith
Jedediah H. Smith
Jefferson Randolph Smith
Klondike Smith
Liz Smith
Lucy Mack Smith
Maggie Smith
Mr. & Mrs. Smith
P. K. Smith
Reggie Smith
Robert, Bob, and Bobby Smith
Sammi Smith
Skyrocket Smith
Snuffy Smith
Soapy Smith
Sonny Smith
William, Bill, Billy, Will, and Willie Smith
Worthington Curtis Smith
Dr. Zachary Smith
Alias Smith & Jones

Really and truly the surname makes no difference, it is the first or Christian name that counts, that is what makes one be as they are.

Delilah. Joe. Penelope. Perrigrine, Sojourner, Ulysses.

Name any name and then remember everybody you ever knew who bore that name. Are they all alike. I think so.

Josef Albers
Josephine Baker
Joe Blow
Joseph Campbell
Joseph Conrad
Joseph Cotton
Chief Joseph
Joe Cocker
Joe DiMaggio
G.I. Joe
Hans Josephus
Joseph Goebbels
Joe Henderson
Shoeless Joe Jackson
Joey Ramone
Joseph McCarthy
José Martí
Josef Stalin
Joseph Merrick
Joseph Ratzinger
Joseph Haydn
Joseph Heller
Joseph of Arimethea
Joseph, Oregon
Joseph, Utah
Joe the Plumber
Joseph Rockefeller
Saint Joe
Giuseppe Verdi
José Zapatero

Can you see why this brings us again to religion. Names and religion are always connected just like that. Nobody interferes between names and religion.

O Ulysses. O Joe. If you claim to be nobody, what appears is your rising up above the commonplace.

Do you begin to see a little what America is what American religion is what American war is. Ulysses S. Grant. General Joe Smith.

Everyman is a type of no man. The boss of his own nowhere. In general heroic.

Would be president. Would be king.

On April 24, 1844, Josiah Quincy and Charles Francis Adams left Boston for the western frontier of their States.

They traveled the upper Mississippi on the steamboat Amaranth and on May 15 arrived knee-deep on a mud road leading to Nauvoo, Ill.

It was thought that Mr. Quincy and Mr. Adams had been mistakenly believed to be—or to be traveling with—a former president.

Mr. Smith, unshaven, wearing *carpenters' pants and a linen jacket,* offered Mr. Adams his blessing and greeted Mr. Quincy with *that sort of cordiality with which the president of a college might welcome a deserving janitor.*

They were led into a house where doors opened and shut on rooms that seemed to be filled with sleeping women. This is what the visitors said.

When they couldn't find a private room, they settled in the parlor. Was this a performance? By whom.

They referred to Mr. Smith as a *bourgeois Mohammed* possessed of a *kingly faculty* with which he collected weak-minded followers.

In the parlor, he opened a cabinet to reveal what they referred to as "curiosities": a recently acquired mummy and some pieces of parchment, after which they were encouraged to pay the elder Mrs. Smith a quarter of a dollar.

Count the bodies in the room. At whose expense is any story told.

Liberty Jail
Independence, MO
Harmony, PA
Bountiful, UT

GEN. SMITH'S VIEWS ON THE GO-VERNMENT AND POLICY OF THE U.S.

I ever feel a double anxiety

like Daniel's
when I view the condition
throughout the world
where

all are created equal
with certain
unalienable rights·

but
some two or three millions of
people are held as slaves for life

and hundreds of our own kindred for a
supposed infraction
be incarcerated in dungeon
glooms
while the
duellist, the debauchee, and the defaulter for
millions, take the upper-
most rooms at feasts

When the boy was no longer a boy, his people was large enough to turn a state's politics, whether of Ohio or Missouri or Illinois.

He ran for president on a platform that argued against the class- and race-based punishments of the state and for the abolition both of slavery and of prisons.

He did not think the number or age of the women to whom he was bound in public or in private was the business of a nation that could barely hold itself together.

He made questionable decisions. He printed money. His stories filled with contradictions.

In his late but not yet latter times, Mr. Smith was often in the wind, slipping out of windows to find a horse kept at the ready. Or running through the woods like a figure illuminated by Experience.

Eventually he was sacked by a posse and placed in a cart from which someone heard him say: *I go as a lamb to the slaughter.*

He was brought indeed to a brick building already smelling of metal and of blood.

When he sat with his brothers, he opened the book he wrote to see what to do now.

But the characters had returned into a language he no longer understood, line after line going nowhere, a labyrinth with no way out.

Beneath the atomic sun, metal touched powder and powder sparked a fire that sent metal out to rake the air, and the body that flew out onto the ground was not a lamb at all but an unwinged bird propped against a wall, full of lead.

When *Brigham Young: Frontiersman* hit the big screen in 1940, Daryl Zanuck was working with a church that wanted to normalize its past toward an assimilated future, but the star of the show is not who you think.

Tyrone Power and Linda Darnell play early converts in love who barely catch a wagon west. Mary Astor and Jean Rogers are the aristocratic wives of Dean Jagger's badly coiffed and doughy Mr. Young.

Mr. Smith is played by a luminous Vincent Price, who looks and sounds like a soft-spoken Thoreau. He's not hiding bodies in a house of wax, but he's magnetized in a way that's not quite right either.

Still, as I watch Mr. Smith throw an axe into a tree, I think I catch a glimpse of what some people saw. A boy inside a man who'll take down everything he knows to make a house he can't yet see.

I was reaching for a passage to the world they came from, the bodies slowly turning in the dirt from which I came.

A sentence shot with sleeplessness.

Something in the middle distance while my eyes are on the road.

I feel for a pen somewhere above the speed limit, clothed in metal flying just above the ground.

I write this sentence on a cliff above a lake.

A deer comes to look while I take something to get me through the twilight.

I write this as I carry its anonymity into the world.

I write it while the Atlantic flyway cries above my head.

I harry it on paths unmade by human passage.

I write it from the audience while silenced by the stage.

Long after the Xs have faded from the pages made of skin.

We are taking part in an eternal order, wrote Anni Albers as the spool ran out. We wander through their ruled lines and shelter in the trees.

This is how we leap from the fire to what comes next.

That's how long the shadow falls.

The voice Augustine heard said "Read."

The voice the boy heard said "Hear."

Write this down.

Both roads led to Carthage.

When the spirit in Mr. Smith fell to earth like an enormous bird, it took time for Mr. Young to find his way among the arguing multitudes empowered by the doctrine of personal revelation. To lobby for the tight-fitting wardrobe, to let out the seams and shorten the appendages, to name the animal whose power he wished to emulate, whose language he wished to speak.

There is never sufficient proof or logic to make sense of what appears in the distance.

Belief and delusion are in the eye of the beholder and in her heart and in his mouth and all their congress.

The story of what happened next may have come from Mr. Young as he whispered into a woman's ear.

He may have so positioned himself in alignment with the sun that someone would be bound to see a light falling on him like a mantle and his hair like a mane and his voice of a sudden like a carnivorous roar. A sound in the imperative with only one meaning.

It came from a creature who did not like the sound of women speaking words he did not understand. And that would eventually be that.

^we are^ in Missouria on a branch of lones creek [ ] Br Brigham
came up with his company driving his ^team^ in the rain and
mud to his knes as happy as a king here we camped the men
went some to browsing the cattle some to cutting wood &
burning coal we got supper went to bed and it soon began to
thunder and lighten and the ^rain^ came faster than ever about
2 oclock in the morning I was caled for to go back two miles
it then snowed I rode behind the man through mud and water
some of the way belly deep to the horse I found the sister that I
was caled to in an old log cabin her child was born before I got
there she had rode 13 miles after she was in travail crosed the
creek on a log after dark her husband carried over such things as
was nessesary left his waggons and teams on the other side as the
water had carried of the bridge, tuesday 7 the ground froze some
I got on to the horse on a mans sadle rode home to our waggon
the creeks had raised ^6feet^ the mud froze the man went
on foot with me I got home safe it came of fair Br Rocwood
brought in some wild ionions and priari flowers

MRS. SESSIONS, HER BOOK

If she or her sister were in a certain way, she wanted a midwife. Someone who didn't start by covering her with a sheet.

Maybe the doctor had only practiced on a horse, maybe he had a past.

If someone had to run to tell of a disaster, the person was already dead, or would be. If she had a horse, she had a chance.

The writing of a letter was an occasion. A hat was an occasion. A poem was an occasion of speech addressing an occasion.

It was safer to tell the story than to write it on paper. Someone might decipher its marks but another would pretend they were meaningless so as not to look unschooled.

Turn the feeling from portrait into landscape: shapes made of time as well as space. Histories told in languages you may or may not understand.

Someone will place alien symbols on a sign. Someone will put their own name on a map. People will drive their cars on roads that one day will cease to exist.

Run the sequence in reverse. Watch the wind wash over their tracks with Nevadan sand. The road insulting that ancient shore: folded over, taken down into an insoluble past.

The sound of metal rails, taken up, melted back into the earth.

THE SNOWS OF YESTERYEAR

While the others were going into raptures about the stars, she felt that she could see her family in the sky, her beloved family, and realized that she was bidding them farewell.

César Aira, tr. Chris Andrews

Miss Snow was born in January. She enters the poem from the east because that's the way it wrote her.

When she looked up from western Massachusetts into heaven, she didn't see stars, she saw faces.

She didn't see a man with a beard, she saw a mother and a father.

Why would a god who could do anything he pleased decide to live alone?

Every surface was written on if you knew how to read.

When the wind was in her ear, the prairie was talking.

She loved the sound of words as they hit the surface of the world. She felt their roots in the dirt she walked on.

She loved to dip a goose feather into a bottle of iron gall ink and watch the feather pull her hand across the page.

She would sometimes fall into a *brown study*.

Her first poem, "Pity &c," appeared in 1825 in the *Western Courier* of Ravenna, Ohio.

The word comes from the Latin, from piety. It meant *to have one's sympathies displaced*.

*

Miss Snow wanted to be loved by multitudes and remain a mystery. She wanted to be *useful as a writer, and unknown as an author*.

To disappear and reappear in distant places, in the clothing of a poem.

She did not want to be married for time and all eternity to the poems of Eliza Snow or Eliza Smith or Eliza Young. She wanted her words to belong to the air.

She would place a veil between the girl whose feather scratched the page and the proper name set in lead and printed in a newspaper that could attract the admiration or disdain of her neighbors.

A name could be a veil. A title could be a fiction.

She became Tullia, Minerva, Cordelia, Fidelity, Narcissa, Pocahontas.

After following the congressional debates that led to the Indian Removal Act of 1830, "Pocahontas" wrote a poem that was printed under the title "The Indian's Song."

The poem appeared in the Ohio *Star* a week before Miss Snow's future husband preached the first service of his new church.

In 1865, when he was dead, she revised the poem, calling it "The Lamanite," the name he had given to an imaginary poet's imaginary tribe.

*

They had come from Sharon, from Becket; had left the failing fabrics of their childhoods to write a new *Exodus* on this hem of a riverbank.

They trusted desire as a kind of revelation. They believed in the momentum of a poem.

They believed there could be a kind of union that meant everyone gave up everything for everyone else.

If they believed in sharing anything, they believed in the explosion of the nuclear family. They believed that theology could dissolve, gracefully, into civic power.

Some truths were more complicated than history cared to say. "We" was a people. "We" was a marriage whose borders were infinitely far away.

They believed in wives who made shirts and wives who were bed-ridden; wives who had other husbands and wives who loved each other; wives who produced nothing but words.

*

When Eliza or Tullia or Cordelia published her first poem in 1825, had she read "The Revolt of Islam" or "Prometheus Unbound" or the lyrics of Percy Shelley's 1824 *Posthumous Poems*?

Did she know that Mary Shelley was Percy's second wife, that she had run away with him in 1814? That their romance was both secret and public, that their marriage was an experiment that included others, that they had to flee their own country in order to perform a household they believed in? That his first wife committed suicide when they returned?

When, as a teenager at the Portage County Fair, Miss Snow won first prize for the best handmade Leghorn hat, did she know of its origin in Livorno, where Mary and Percy lived briefly in an unacknowledged union in 1818?

Had she or her future husband, read *A Defence of Poetry* or the *Masque of Anarchy*? Or Mary Shelley's *Frankenstein*; or *Mathilda*, her novelistic parable of toxic obedience?

Rise, Shelley wrote, *like lions after slumber.*

Did it seem that events might be driven by poetic necessity, that there were laws above the law?

Poets, this one said, *are the hierophants of an unapprehended inspiration; the mirrors of the gigantic shadows which futurity casts upon the present; the words which express what they understand not; the trumpets which sing to battle and feel not what they inspire; the influence which is moved not but moves.*

A prophet or poet was called to represent an invisible world within the visible, the fuse of imagination inside the movement of public events.

Poets are the unacknowledged legislators of the world.

In 1842 one writer married another. She was a record keeper who understood the laws of encryption. He was a translator, a lightning rod, a general, an already married man who was about to run for president.

They dwelt across the Atlantic, in Possibility.

*

In the late 1830s, Mr. Smith called Miss Snow to serve as the church's poet.

Later, *Times and Seasons* published her poem declaring the existence of a mother in heaven.

Her husband had been shot, but she could see him in the sky. She would place an image of herself sitting next to him.

No one ever talked about the legislative function of the poem.

*

Miss Snow wrote poems for her friends, she lay her hands on them and prophesied their futures. She and Mrs. Sessions were regular healers married forever to the same man.

They recorded their visits with each other and with Mr. Smith. They spoke in an unbreakable code, full of elisions.

When they gathered other women to taste the gifts of the spirit, you could hear their unsupervised joy.

Miss Snow moved into a bedroom next to Emma's.

Mrs. Sessions made Joseph a shirt.

They both held on to certain understandings, knowing in private they must deny them in public.

They were Mrs. Smith.

*

Miss Snow's husband's first wife had not committed suicide. Together Emma Hale Smith and Eliza Roxcy Snow denied the unions and displacements that were happening in the upper rooms.

Together they went to the governor of Illinois. They did not ask the governor to release them from bondage.

They did not offer the governor a defense of polygamy; they denied its existence. They did not discuss the subject of a "higher law." They asked him to protect their husband and his people.

Miss Hale of Harmony, Penna. had followed Mr. Smith to Palmyra and Kirtland and to Nauvoo, the city which he said meant *a beautiful plantation.*

From this muddy lowland, he preached against slavery and started an army. He borrowed money. He invested badly. He improvised a system of communal wealth.

He revealed that his god had required him to marry other women. He depended on the kindness of strangers and friends. He built a mansion with many bedrooms.

A beautiful plantation meant different things to different women. Scarlet. Sojourner. Sally. Emma. Eliza. Jane. Augusta.

*

Eliza Snow had left the eastern States for an unmapped bedroom in Illinois.

When her husband died who was not her husband in the eyes of Illinois, she married Brigham Young but only for her time on earth, not the afterlife.

Some say this was in 1846. Some say it was later in the part of Mexico belonging mainly to the Utes, which became Utah Territory.

For a while, Eliza lived there with her white sister-in-law and a Pahvant Ute woman named Sally, who was said, among the Snows and Youngs, to have been saved from a murderous trafficker.

There is no way to speak of Sally, which is not her name, without using the words of others.

At first, they slept on the ground or on a kind of willow lattice extending from the walls of a log house.

In 1855 they moved into the many-gabled lodging called the Lion House.

Downstairs Miss Snow sat at the lion's right hand at dinner and at prayers.

Some think Sally too became a Mrs. Young, some think she was as captive in the Lion House as she'd been before. Some said she hid there under the protection of other women. From a distance, the categories of indentured and familial labor blur, their clarity, if it ever existed, lost.

In Nauvoo, Eliza Snow had been called High Priestess. She was Governess, Secretary, Editor, Poet, Singer, Prophetess, Counselor, Interpreter.

In Salt Lake City, she was called Miss Snow. She was called Sister Smith. She was called Presidentess.

*

A few weeks before Miss Snow's death, Arthur Conan Doyle's first Sherlock Holmes adventure arrived in print.

Study in Scarlet was an exposé of the coercive deviance of Mormon polygamy and the violence of its territorial theocracy.

It appeared in *Beeton's 1887 Christmas Annual*. The issue would become the most expensive magazine in the world.

Doyle wrote his *Study in Scarlet* just after the height of the Mormon Emigration movement.

In the mid-19th century, there were twice as many believers in Britain as there were in the Utah Territory.

While Miss Snow heard the prairie speaking with the voice of gods, Doyle heard only silence when he put his ear to the surface of the trans-Atlantic page.

*

Ralph Waldo Emerson, Abraham Lincoln, Henry Wadsworth Longfellow, Susan B. Anthony, Victor Hugo, Alfred Lord Tennyson, Charles Dickens, Queen Victoria.

These were signatures she had collected in her book.

In the early 1870s, she traveled to Europe, northern Africa, and Palestine with other members of the church's upper hierarchy including her brother Lorenzo, who was eventually named the church's prophet.

Accounts of their travels bear a notable resemblance to Sir Richard F. Burton's ethnographic writing about the peculiar white people of Utah a decade earlier.

Eliza Roxcy Snow Smith Young died in December of 1887. Her life moved into tiny print at the bottom of the front page of the *New York Times.*

Her stone in Brigham Young's private cemetery, a block from the center of the Mormon world, reads:

SACRED TO THE MEMORY
of
ELIZA R. SNOW SMITH
Born in Becket, Berkshire Co., Mass.
JAN. 21, 1804:
DIED
At Salt Lake City, Utah.
DEC. 5, 1887

She had, at that time, been married to Mr. Young for thirty-eight years. She had been presiding at the Lion House for thirty-two.

She had placed her hand in the mouth of a lion when she was a child and had learned to live among them.

Scan the stone for a *memory of snow*, for *snow* falling across the white marble into *salt*, the arc of *memory* opening like a mouth that shows a key on its tongue: *of.*

Who this ground belongs to. Who belongs to this ground.

MATOAKA & MRS. ROLFE

Ideology may appear clean to its proponents as long as it remains abstract, but when it is put into practice it takes the shape of a crime.

Mahmoud Darwish, tr. Ibrahim Muhawi

The daughter of Powhaten did not publish poems under the name Pocahontas. She didn't write "An Indian's Song." Nor did she appear, in the extant record, to consider herself or her people lost.

Though she did, according to some accounts, defend the life of a certain colonial by the name of Smith.

It was said by Mr. Smith that when the girl's father Powhaten, the *mamanatowick*, who through his maternal lineage possessed the authority among his people to knock the brains out of anyone he chose with a single stroke or to require others to do so on his behalf, but who had in this case, according to Smith, raised his weapon to kill him personally, Pocahontas his daughter lay her head against this Smith and thereby saved it from removal, linking her fate to his.

When she was captured by the English six years later, she changed her name, or someone else did, to Rebecca.

In the unrelenting algebra of conquest, women may be passed back and forth across imaginary lines; they may be translated from one system into another.

Alexander Whitaker, a minister in the town where the girl whom Mr. Smith called Pocahontas was held hostage, taught her English.

Conversion is language's most powerful performance, according to those who find it in their heart. It turns words into evidence (signage) of things not seen (signifiers).

It is the bringing of something into existence by saying it is so. I am a man. Let there be light.

It is the lifting of one thing to reveal what is underneath. Then covering it back up.

The speaking of a word itself enacts a species of faith. Do you hear me?

Like Mary Jemison and Mary Rowlandson, the person referred to as Pocahontas developed an indelible bond with her captors. A relationship that is impossible, even now, to name. Like Mrs. Jemison, she stayed.

She was described by John Smith as a girl of ten around six or seven years before she married her second husband, a white man named John Rolfe.

When Mr. Rolfe wrote to the governor of his plantation asking permission to marry a girl, a Powhaten princess, his first-nation hostage, he described their relationship as an entanglement of thought.

His request was not, he said, founded in *carnal affection* but an enthrallment by which he found himself *in so intricate a labyrinth* that he *was even a-wearied to unwind* himself *thereout.*

A brief period following the marriage that had put an end to the intricate exhaustion of Mr. Rolfe has been referred to as "The Peace of Pocahontas."

In the ninth month of this peace, Mrs. Rolfe gave birth to a child who would be known legally as Thomas Rolfe.

In 1616, Mr. Rolfe and Mrs. Rolfe shipped to London where she was exhibited as evidence of the adaptability of the first peoples in the vicinity of Jamestown.

To the court, she was a sample of what empire could do. A specimen whose skin and hair and dress the pink-skinned people sought, almost universally, every opportunity to see and to touch.

This was what the Jamestown investors wanted to argue was a

peaceable union. A match concocted in someone's idea of heaven; a piece of destiny you could buy into.

She sat for a portrait. She danced. She was representative.

By the time Thomas Rolfe was two, she was gone.

In an engraving made the same year by Simon de Passe, she is encircled by words and holding a quill pen. The words tell her lineage and her alias but among them is not the name by which we know her.

When something is on display, something else is hidden.

If I doubt the sincerity of Rebecca's conversion, am I negating her will or recognizing it?

No one had written down when the person said to be Pocahontas was born or what she died of.

She was buried in an unmarked grave in Gravesend just before her husband set sail again.

Her father had dozens of wives, who did not live together. We know almost nothing about her mother.

Because there is no trace of her mother in this story, some historians believe that Matoaka's mother died as her daughter fought her way out from inner sea to outer land and that the girl who lay her head against the cheek of Captain Smith was a motherless child.

Some say the girl's name meant Little Wanton. Others, Playful One.

Mrs. Rolfe had other names before she became Pocahontas. Matoaka is said to mean Bright Stream Between the Hills. Her other name cannot be translated.

The town of Pocahontas, in Pocahontas County, Iowa, is 98.3% white and .1% Native American.

Statistically, the Ioway or Baxoje people no longer exist in the state that took their name a few years after the United States took their land.

For a people to no longer be represented statistically is one way to describe forced displacement and germ warfare.

Peg Mullen, the anti-war activist played by Carol Burnett in the film *Friendly Fire*, was born in Pocahontas to a Catholic family.

Her son was killed by "friendly artillery" operated by soldiers fighting on the same side of the American war against Viet Nam.

When Mrs. Mullen bought space in the *Des Moines Register* and filled it with crosses for dead soldiers, when she refused the medals and the grave marker offered by the US military and returned President Nixon's letter of condolence, and marched against the wars that followed, was she, in effect, touching her son's cheek with her own? Or, like the painting of Mary who oversaw the students of the Sacred Heart school in Pocahontas, was she placing her son's body on her lap and saying here it is, this is what it looks like?

Was she refusing, as Mamie Till did, to bury the body before the public could contemplate its wounds and begin to take in what it had to say? Refusing the privacy of grief, pulling aside the curtain of propriety and pointing.

Look, here is the body. Were you there? Did you see it coming? Where were you when this happened to my son? What you have done to those I love, you do to me. Look me in the eye. Behold.

No one's going anywhere. No one is leaving this room until they see.

What direction does your sentence move: you belonging to the land or the land belonging to you.

This is a question of the people and the state.

What can or cannot be bought and sold, given and taken.

A question and a statement.

In what was called the United Order, there was no selling of crops, no personal gain that wasn't within reach of the greater good. That was the idea.

We look not at the things which are seen but the things which are not seen. Our affliction which is *but for a moment* is attached to *a far more exceeding and eternal weight.*

Feel this weight, even for a moment. Such is the eternal. The stopping of the clock.

When one points behind the shape of one body, there ever is another there.

Where is the line between yours and ours.

Depends on whom you ask. Depends on where you stand.

Rolfe, Iowa, is 1% less white than the town of Pocahontas. Both reside in Pocahontas County in a state named after the Iowa, Ioway, or Baxoje people, a branch of the Ho-Chunk nation.

Some of the peoples native to the land bordered by the Missouri and Big Sioux Rivers on the west and the Mississippi on the east, have family who lived there for about 13,000 years by the settler clock.

Their population began declining in the mid-18th century when they were exposed to the diseases brought by missionaries who preferred not to shoot the people they encountered. In this way their fire could appear friendly while achieving similar effects.

It is written that between 1820 and 1840, the Iowa people ceded their lands in what would become Minnesota, Iowa, and Missouri to the US government and moved to a reservation along the Big Nemaha River.

The difference between moving and being moved is the difference between having the authority to knock out a person's brains with a single stroke and the authority to have one's brains knocked out for any reason.

George Catlin's painting of Iowa Indians visited London and Paris before landing at the National Gallery of Art.

The statue of a woman said to be Pocahontas in a small Iowa town has its right hand extended as if in welcome and its left hand touching its torso above the waist.

If I read this body language, I think she is saying that her job makes her sick.

I think she is saying she is tired of standing up, that this might be the loneliest county in the world.

She looks like she wishes she could take a break, that someone would bring her something to eat, that she had a place to lie down.

She looks like she has stopped wondering if this is what the warring tribes of white people consider an appropriate response to saving their lives.

When Carolyn Jean Spellmann Shoemaker discovered minor
planet number 4487 she gave it the name by which most
people know Mrs. Rolfe. In the sky above Flagstaff, Arizona,
Pocahontas joined the company of Proust and Ramses, Van Gogh,
Mahler, Vermeer, Schumann, Stravinsky, Pascal, Charlieparker,
Asclepius, Jackierobinson, Puccini, Schoenberg, Picasso, Lennon,
McCartney, Harrison, Starr, Ptolemy, Garibaldi, Freud, Bartok,
Dickens, Euclid, and Jimihendrix.

Shoemaker, a seventh-grade school teacher who became
an astronomer when she was in her fifties, had at one time
discovered more heavenly bodies than anyone who had ever lived.

Because Thomas Rolfe, the son of Matoaka or Rebecca, survived long enough to inflict the agonies of childbirth on a woman of his choosing, there eventually came to be a seventh-generation descendant named Glenn Strange, an actor known mostly for his performance as the bartender in *Gunsmoke* and the monster in *Frankenstein* spin-offs after Boris Karloff left the role in the early 1940s.

He appeared as the arch-villainous cop killer Butch Cavendish in *The Lone Ranger*.

He is 6' 5". His biography on the Internet Movie Database refers to him as a *beast of a man*.

In many of his films, including *The Mad Monster* (1942) and *House of Frankenstein* (1944) in which he played the title character, his name doesn't appear in the credits.

In one of the few cast photographs in which Strange appears, he is in the back row, a head above his more famous co-stars. At the center of the staged chaos of the scene, he looks straight at the camera, ready for the close-up that never came.

Consider the trademark illiteracy of Mary Shelley's creature. On film, he is almost always referred to as a monster, although the character Shelley wrote into existence is a highly literate man whose larger-than-life form is reinforced, not diminished, by his rhetorical skill.

In the novel, his status is that of a "creature," a category he shares with other humans.

He manifests far more of what is generally referred to as humanity than the man in the white coat who appears to have pieced together a body out of miscellaneous meats without staining his clothes.

Mr. Strange was born in Weed, Territory of New Mexico, and grew up in Cross Cut, Texas.

According to the Texas State Historical Association, Cross Cut was originally named Cross Out. Founded in 1878 and wrecked by the Depression, the town had 79 people in 1940, 45 in 1980, and 0 in 2000.

What did it mean to be a monster named Strange. To be strange as a child, as an adolescent, as a grown man.

To be a native alien in the heart of the republic of Texas. To come into the klieg lights from a misnamed town that no longer exists.

Here is one of many deformations: to be the exiled native is to be the creature, the monster, the villain.

Consider the body of Glenn Strange strapped to the table in *House of Frankenstein*. Boris Karloff's upward mobility has placed him in a white jacket with his hand on the switch.

Like a god, this white man sits at the border between life and death. Like a narcissistic parent, he feels so certain of the creature's love he's almost bored by it. It has become quaint, picturesque, worthy only of the most fleeting attention.

The subject on the table appears to accept this moment, the moment of the willing sacrifice. If that's what you want.

He looks back at the doctor with indulgence, knowing some will read this as the long-suffering patience of a domesticated creature. He sees the endgame. He knows how the story goes. He understands the master as the master will never understand him.

He looks like Isaac on the altar, Jesus on the cross.

Mary Shelley's primary point of reference, like that of her creature, is Milton's *Paradise Lost*. A story of creation and miscreation, of childhood gone wrong, which becomes an allegory of what happens when men try to reproduce themselves.

It is the story of a motherless child. A man with a limp and a questionable inheritance. A man who is angry with the father who betrayed him.

Consider the appearance of Mr. Strange in *Abbott and Costello Meet Frankenstein*.

His speechlessness is made much of. It never seems to occur to anyone that he may be speaking a language none of them can understand.

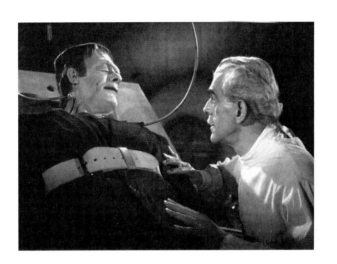

In 1969, the *New York Times* mistakenly printed an image of Glenn Strange in its obituary for Boris Karloff.

In the 1944 *House of Frankenstein*, Karloff has top billing as the mad doctor, and Glenn Strange, whose character dominates the film's publicity, is listed neither on posters nor film trailers.

In some Christian traditions, the father-god is said to have two sons: Lucifer who falls and Jesus who rises.

An origin story among the Paiutes also tells of two sons: one a trusted elder of their nation and the other a greedy young crybaby whose fall produced the white man.

Corrections are not equivalent to repair.

FINDING AID

Slavery Box	Magic Box	American Loyalists Box
Science Box	Medicine Box	Agriculture Box
Societies Box	Poetry Box	Indian Box

UNCATEGORICAL FEELINGS

A name is said to be proper and singular even when hidden behind a patronym.

When Sister Smith came to visit, Sister Smith might record the occasion in her book, but who was it.

Miss Snow was sometimes Smith or Young. Miss Partridge was sometimes Smith or Lyman. The other Miss Partridge was a Smith and a Young. Miss Huntington was sometimes Jacobs and Smith and Young all at once. Augusta was an Adams and a Cobb and a Young, though she married a Smith after he was dead, so she was sisters with her friends with or without Mr. Young.

There is no way to find such a body in the archive without rattling her troubled peace.

Here lies the evidence, here it has joined the ether or the earth. To whom did this fury, this joy or complication occur.

Habeas corpus: show me the body. If you cannot find it, there has been no crime. Where does the body exist that cannot be found.

Matilda Joslyn Gage: *It is sometimes better to be a dead man than a live woman.*

Some part of them has known your mouth. Their carbon and nitrogen has sugared up the grain. You cannot say you have not partaken.

Of what, of this.

The freedoms that passed between women could be both vast and precise. Intentional entanglements voiced and unvoiced.

They might involve the touching of the brow or of the crown, above or below. A woman's arm might reach in to adjust the body inside another where no one else had touched and in this way accomplish her salvation.

The power of such a role, like the power to speak with an authority beyond accident, includes the right to decide where to place the curtain around the scene and who to place upon its stage.

A woman might prophesy on another's fate. This is a structure within which some appear to flourish by speaking, some by being spoken. Some by placing her hands, some by receiving them. Some by walking out the door.

To transmute divine love is to unbind the categories of consensual life through which other forms of life rush into being.

When a married one would marry another who may also be married, is it an expansion or a redefinition. What is its place, in what theater are the words spoken.

One may serve as a proxy or perform an adaptive role in accordance with shifts in venue or of script.

What does it mean for the living to bury the dead, to be among them later on, to marry them on earth, whether they were present or not.

If she married more than one, what names will she take. If she kept her share of proper names, how will you find her.

Is she singular or multiple. Proper or improper.

In the unbounded evolutionary present of a self among others, what is her relation to the other women in the house. As the view is foreshortened by the passage from one time to another, some scenes darken as others are illuminated.

After their father died in 1840, Emily and Eliza Partridge hired out as domestic workers.

Emily: The first door that opened for us was to go to [the] Smiths, which we accepted. [...] Joseph and Emma were almost like a mother and father.

Later Mr. Smith married first one, then the other sister.

In May 1843, William Clayton wrote:

> Prest [Smith] stated to me that he had had a little trouble with sis E[mma]. he was asking E[liza] Partridge concerning Jackson conduct during Prest. absence & E[mma] came up stairs. He shut to the door not knowing who it was and held it. She came to the door & called Eliza 4 times & tried to force open the door. Prest. opened it & told her the cause etc. She seemed much irritated.

In many stories Emma Smith's position shifts between sister and malevolent resister of the draft into polygamy.

It was rumored that Mrs. Smith pushed the pregnant Eliza down the stairs. Most people thought that meant the poet Eliza Snow but some thought it was Miss Eliza Partridge.

One door opened. Another Prest shut.

MISS FANNY ALGER, MRS. SMITH, MRS. CUSTER

MISS LUCINDA PENDLETON, MRS. HARRIS, MRS. SMITH

MISS LOUISA BEAMAN, MRS. SMITH, MRS. YOUNG

MISS ZINA DIANTHA HUNTINGTON, MRS. JACOBS,
MRS. SMITH, MRS. YOUNG

MISS PRESENDIA LATHROP HUNTINGTON, MRS. BUELL,
MRS. SMITH, MRS. KIMBALL

MISS AGNES MOULTON COOLBRITH, MRS. SMITH,
MRS. SMITH, MRS. SMITH, MRS. PICKETT

MISS PATTY BARTLETT, MRS. SESSIONS, MRS. SMITH,
MRS. PARRY

MISS SYLVIA PORTER SESSIONS, MRS. LYONS, MRS. SMITH,
MRS. KIMBALL, MRS. CLARK

MISS MARY ELIZABETH ROLLINS, MRS. LIGHTNER,
MRS. SMITH, MRS. YOUNG

MISS MARINDA NANCY JOHNSON, MRS. HYDE, MRS. SMITH

MISS ELIZABETH DAVIS, MRS. GOLDSMITH, MRS.
BRACKENBURY, MRS. DURFEE, MRS. SMITH, MRS. LOTT

MISS SARAH MARYETTE KINGSLEY, MRS. HOWE,
MRS. CLEVELAND, MRS. SMITH, MRS. SMITH

MISS DELCENA DIADAMIA JOHNSON, MRS. SHERMAN,
MRS. SMITH, MRS. BABBITT

MISS ALMERA WOODWARD JOHNSON, MRS. SMITH,
MRS. BARTON

MISS ELIZA ROXCY SNOW, MRS. SMITH, MRS. YOUNG

MISS SARAH ANN WHITNEY, MRS. SMITH, MRS. KINGSBURY,
MRS. KIMBALL

MISS MARTHA MCBRIDE, MRS. KNIGHT, MRS. SMITH,
MRS. KIMBALL

MISS RUTH DAGGET VOSE, MRS. SAYERS, MRS. SMITH

MISS FLORA ANN WOODWORTH, MRS. SMITH, MRS. GOVE

MISS EMILY DOW PARTRIDGE, MRS. SMITH, MRS. YOUNG

MISS ELIZA MARIA PARTRIDGE, MRS. SMITH, MRS. LYMAN

MISS LUCY WALKER, MRS. SMITH, MRS. KIMBALL

MISS SARAH LAWRENCE, MRS. SMITH, MRS. KIMBALL,
MRS. MOUNT

MISS MARIA LAWRENCE, MRS. SMITH, MRS. YOUNG,
MRS. BABBIT

MISS HELEN MAR KIMBALL, MRS. SMITH, MRS. WHITNEY

MISS HANNAH S. ELLIS, MRS. SMITH

MISS ELVIRA ANNIE COWLES, MRS. HOLMES, MRS. SMITH

MISS RHODA RICHARDS, MRS. SMITII, MRS. YOUNG

MISS DESDEMONA CATLIN WADSWORTH FULLMER,
MRS. SMITH, MRS. BENSON, MRS. MCLANE

MISS OLIVE GREY FROST, MRS. SMITH, MRS. YOUNG

MISS MELISSA LOTT, MRS. SMITH, MRS. BERNHISEL,
MRS. WILLES

MISS NANCY MARIA WINCHESTER, MRS. SMITH,
MRS. KIMBALL, MRS. ARNOLD

MISS FANNY YOUNG, MRS. CARR, MRS. MURRAY, MRS. SMITH

There is no contemporary record of what did and didn't happen when Miss Snow lived in Missouri at the time the extermination of Mormons was ordered by a governor Mr. Boggs.

A cousin later whispered she'd been raped by an anti-Mormon mob, but on this subject her own records are silent.

Her world was on fire, and fire is full of untranslatable words.

If boys are killed for their beliefs, their spiritual fate is a rising up. If girls or women survive their assaults, their status is hidden, ambiguated, or displayed for further punishment.

The fact that Miss Snow had no children has been interpreted in many ways. Some say she was pregnant by Mr. Smith but Mrs. Smith pushed her down the stairs and she miscarried.

It is a commonplace to find her described as *curiously virginal.*

The imperative to explain, the need to prove or define, may in itself be disciplinary.

Her agency in most matters is seldom addressed except when it resembles conformity.

From a distance she appears to have preferred the company of women, intimately and publicly.

Attachments of many kinds may function simultaneously as a constraint and an expansion of biographical possibility. She sometimes referred to her *female family.*

Most of the poems she wrote didn't fit neatly into the categories named in her published volumes: Religious, Political, Historical. Many were addressed to specific people, mostly women, some famous, mostly friends. They often took an epistolary form that, like the poems of Sister Augusta Adams Cobb, bore a resemblance to prophecy.

However these poems functioned aesthetically or devotionally, they were also legislative: emotionally binding and legally non-binding, not nuptial and not unnuptial, verbal records of uncategorized sensations and alliances, sites of self-invention, pledges of allegiance that could leap between body and spirit, the earthly and the eternal.

> To Mrs. Stenhouse in Switzerland
> To Mrs. Marion R. Pratt on the Death of her Little One
> Inscribed to Sister Howard
> To All the Ladies Who Reside in the 2d Mansion of Prest. B. Young
> To Alice G. Heywood
> To Mrs. Ellen S. Clawson in Memory of Her Little Daughter Florence, Aged 15 Months, Who Was Accidentally Scalded So Severely as to Cause Death
> Parting Lines to Mrs. S. M.W.
> To Mrs. Mary Pratt on the Death of Her Little Son
> To Mrs. Sylvia P. Lyon on the Death of Her Little Daughter
> Lines for Mrs. Wooley's Album
> Acrostic for Anna Geen
> To Queen Victoria

Her pseudonyms included Angerona and Camera Obscura.

She sometimes signed her poems *incog.*

Mrs. Sessions in her diary took note of the poems addressed to her and to her daughter Sylvia. Here was evidence. Let the record show.

Miss Snow's poem to Sarah Melissa Grange Kimball begins:

Sarah, I love you —I have loved you long.

Where does not-knowing touch the sovereignties of poetry and personhood. Where does the right to obscurity meet institutionalized silence.

It meant something to them. It means something to me. That is what the existence of the poem says into the historical dark.

A feeling may have a provenance beyond category or may be categorical without naming names.

A poem may serve as witness to the invisible as it becomes materially real. To speak at the risk of being propelled outside the boundaries of one's own known world. To enact the relation that occupies one's very mouth.

This is the performative power that enabled Augusta Cobb to prophesy to a prophet.

It gives friendships, like marriages, an afterlife. Uncategorically.

Eliza Roxcy Snow and Zina Diantha Huntington were baptized citizens of Zion in 1835.

They sometimes worked as a spiritual team, speaking in tongues and interpreting each other.

Moved by an unseen hand, breathed out by an unseen voice, singing words not their own, that flew through the body like a new dance.

They outdid and unmade themselves. They became a sound somewhere else.

They fell asleep in one place and woke up in another. They were translated.

A marriage without issue may yet produce couplets.

Once a woman produced a book from her skirt.

She called it her *hideous progeny.*

When Zina Diantha Huntington was seven months pregnant by Mr. Jacobs, she was sealed to Mr. Smith.

After Mr. Smith's death, Mr. Jacobs was told that Mrs. Jacobs no longer belonged to him.

Having been Mrs. Smith, she and her possessions were by negotiation shared with Mr. Young. Mr. Jacobs was witness to her third marriage.

In Utah, Zina and Eliza continued to speak in languages that were and were not understood.

Eliza founded the *Woman's Exponent*, where arguments for women's suffrage and catalogs of women's patents and news of women around the world were printed next to impassioned defenses of polygamy and arguments for the political autonomy of the Territory.

Zina became president of the Church Silk Association. She traveled the territory promoting the cultivation of mulberry trees and silkworms. She managed Brigham Young's cocoonery.

Mr. Young preached that resisters would not be tolerated.

Mrs. Young wrote that a woman *must regard her husband with indifference.*

Many were sent away as fishers of men and harvesters of women. Most of these went more than once into the fields, not of wheat or corn but of the spirit and the book. It all sounded quite natural.

Some spent more years in the fields than at home.

Those who were left governed. Or those who governed stayed.

The houses left behind by fishermen and harvesters were often filled with women and children.

What is the exception and what is the rule. Some at home found forms of love stronger than their feelings for the absent patriarch.

Some like Mrs. Sessions could not abide another wife. Some divorced. Some found all their options impossible.

Q: You claim to have married Joseph Smith?
A: No, I do not claim any such thing; he married me. The Lord told him to take me and he did so.

Q: After your separation from Mr. Jacobs, whom did you marry?
A: I married my father. My mother died, and I went to keep house for my father.

Q: How, then could you have been sealed to Joseph Smith without first having heard the doctrine of plural marriage?
A: Joseph Smith sent my brother Dimick to explain it to me.

Arranged as music

the woman

behind the man

behind the curtain

is transposed

as the opposite

of herself

To be flowered

on earth as

to be sacked

in a kitchen

Prey is just

something pretty

in the distance

that cannot

in a story

be easily

removed

The way she holds

his knife

the way he sings

off-key

Eliza Snow's vision of family as a structure beyond history—one that had both a pre-existence and an afterlife—included the belief that friendship was part of such a family.

Her editors note she felt a "kinship" with other women who were sealed to Joseph Smith.

Such kinship, bound neither by blood nor by law, is rooted in recognition and attention. Its processes are laid bare upon a face.

What happens when a relationship framed as rivalry is converted into a coalition.

Ruth May Fox, a poet who stepped into Miss Snow's footprints, agreed that a mother-in-heaven was sitting overhead. Matilda Teasdale backed her up in her address "To the Young Ladies." The story had an intergenerational life.

Official history places Mr. Smith's prophetic doctrine before the composition of Miss Snow's poem, but it is unclear if the doctrine would have existed without the women who surrounded its genesis.

If Miss Snow and Mrs. Fox and Mrs. Teasdale had it right, the final judgment at which you are asked to report for your doings will not take place in palatial or judicial courts or in the boardroom or onscreen.

It will not be enhanced with a diaphanous wardrobe. You will not report as a worker to the boss but as a child to your parents, called to account by the terrifying bonds of the familial.

What on earth have you done?

This logic, Miss Snow's poem says, is self-evident. I have addressed the mother, I have asked her a question. She exists.

Mothering translates reproductive calculus into social welfare and sequestered power.

Not the angel but the goddess. Not the servant but the queen. Divinely unreachable. Busy as hell.

A friend is the one with whom you share everything else.

Many males and many females live together in the same flower.

So wrote Erasmus Darwin in 1791, while arguing for the abolition of slavery and for the education of young women.

It may seem a solecism in language to call a flower which contains many of both sexes an individual; and the more so to call a tree or shrub an individual, which consists of so many flowers.

This is where an Enlightenment human begins to meet the language of other species.

Form is not destiny. Not in plants. Nor other bodies. Corporal or governmental.

Nature is not governed by categorical norms only described by them as patterns of greater or lesser variation from the curve.

Never, wrote Darwin's grandson Charles while the war against the imagination raged on, *say higher or lower.*

In common 19th-century American parlance these were polygamy and slavery.

To Matilda Joslyn Gage, co-author of the *Declaration of the Rights of Women* and the *History of Women's Suffrage*, the twins were, rather, Church and State.

Bodies used toward different ends while legislation categorically offers white men full humanity with all the attendant privileges of dogma and of law.

In *Women, Church, and State*, Mrs. Gage argues that John Milton's greatest but not only crime was to turn the desire for exploitation into poetic form.

Mrs. Gage was as primary in the fight for women's rights as Mrs. Stanton and Mrs. Anthony.

She could see that Haudenosaunee democracy was far better for women than what US Christianity allowed.

If you don't know her name, it's because she was an atheist.

The Matilda Effect is what ails you when you are deemed unfit for the public and others are credited for your work.

Mrs. Gage's son-in-law was L. Frank Baum. Some credit her with imagining an alternate universe in which a curtain opens and patriarchal power is exposed.

In 1870 Mormon women gathered in Salt Lake City to protest the US House of Representatives' passage of the Cullom Bill, which would allow the confiscation of Mormon property and imprison polygamous men.

Indignation takes many forms.

This one got the attention of the women's rights movement in the area of New York State burned over by Mr. Sullivan but not yet divided by the Eisenhower highway system between Rochester and Syracuse.

The women in the tabernacle were defending polygamy while arguing, as they had in print, for women's suffrage, two issues commonly seen as in conflict.

The meeting was organized by leaders of the Relief Society, the women's organization that began in the early church and that Brigham Young had sought to disband after his wagons were unloaded in the land of the people referred to as the Utes.

Polygamy could look different from the inside. Some women were married with other women to the same man. Some were simultaneously married to more than one man.

Who belonged to the captivity and who wrote it. This is a problem that cannot be unknotted.

Some returned from their wrestling with another, the same in one sense, altered in another.

I love Miss Margaret Curtis who, after leaving home for a Mr. Shipp, with whom she became unhappy, left again, went to medical school, practiced obstetrics, and remarried the younger Mr. Roberts.

Of those who married a Smith or a Young, some stayed, some left, and some of it went unrecorded.

At least ten of Mr. Young's wives formally divorced him. Some chose to leave the territory entirely.

MISS MANNING & MRS. JAMES

God is change.

Octavia Butler

Jane Manning was born into a family of domestic servants in Connecticut sometime in the early 1820s.

There were no laws as yet governing child labor or education, whatever your year, your color, your name.

Sometime around the age of sixteen or seventeen, the child was with child.

There's no record of a finger pointing at her adolescent belly the way an angel pointed at Mary's with the unanaesthetized tip of a gold-leafed Italian arrow.

The boy could have been a love child covered by a story. Could have been an intergenerational abuse of power. Which boy. Either one.

When she knew what was happening to her we don't know if she looked enraptured or aghast, agonized or fulfilled.

These are not the only options.

She bore a boy child and named him Sylvester without naming his father. Some said the man was a traveling preacher. Some a French Canadian. Could have been both.

Miss Manning professed her faith and was baptized into the New Canaan Congregational Church a few years later.

She was rebaptized into Mormonism the year after that.

Three weeks after her second baptism, she heard herself speaking in tongues and frightened up the house.

The lines between fear and mystery, violence and ambiguity, devotion and belonging pulsed in and out of focus.

BY WHAT MEANS CAME JANE UNTO
THE BEAUTIFUL PLANTATION

A missionary named Wandell had brought the word to Norwalk and Wilton and New Canaan.

Soon after, he was saying Zion was gathering further out. A new book was rewriting the old one. Both books involved sojourns in the *wilderness*.

Mr. Wandell convinced Miss Manning to pack her best clothes. So she took her four-year-old boy, her mother, her surviving siblings, and a pony-skin trunk on the inland road with Wandell and some other of his converts.

Sometime around the crossing of Lake Erie or the arrival in Cleveland, either Miss Manning was required to pay more money than she had or she was told she could not continue without papers proving she was free.

The paler ones continued on. That is, they offered to carry Miss Manning's things and left her and her people to continue on hostile ground by foot.

None of the pale ones in the company seem to have understood what it meant to cross over into land where those who resembled Miss Manning could be taken as fugitives unless they could prove otherwise.

When her rough-pegged shoes wore out, she walked barefoot by night to western Illinois, where the town of Nauvoo was still being hammered to the soggy eastern bank of the Mississippi River.

Wandell and the others, who had taken the pony-skin trunk that held everything Miss Manning couldn't carry in her arms, continued by boat and by stage through Ohio.

Somewhere along the way the trunk and its contents were lost or sold or left behind, and Miss Manning arrived in the city of Mr. Smith without work or lodging or a trunk full of clothes.

She was trained in the labors of domestic service, but the city at which she arrived shoeless was a city of women looking for the same work.

Some men were repeatedly sent out on missions, some were soldiers or farmers, pharmacists or shopkeepers, some were cast out or wandered off on their own, but women were everywhere.

Miss Manning's account of arriving in Nauvoo is dominated by her recognition of a Smith whose face she had seen in a revelation of her own.

After she told Mr. Smith of her missing trunk, Mr. Wandell was convicted of unchristian behavior toward *certain colored brethren* he had abandoned in Cleveland, but it is not clear if he was excommunicated or fined.

Mr. and Mrs. Smith brought Miss Manning into the large house that also served as the town's best hotel.

She stayed in the wing with the other household workers, some of whom confided that they were wives of the proprietor, living there both as laborers and as family.

What appealed to the teenage woman about Wandell's message?

Its vision of lateral relations and shared fate, with no paid clergy and only the Divine above? A biblical transit from segregated worship to a church that promised otherwise, where her gifts and her voice had a place?

Everyone in the new town would be a brother or a sister; even a priest was neither reverend nor father. Every brother and sister was a servant to each other in a union, where property or *increase* were held in common.

Servitude replaced with service and mutual aid.

Service was to be the condition of all believers, with sacrifices counterbalanced by the equal and opposite force of agency. Those who had authority washed and anointed others.

Power was power of the spirit, which was free, without quotation marks. Revelation was daily improvisatory practice among the patterns of domestic and civic life.

In 1844, Mr. and Mrs. Smith, then in their forties, asked Jane, who was in her twenties, if she would like to be adopted into their family.

In a layered system of material, filial, sexual, and spiritual relations, it is impossible to know what the question meant to the one who spoke it or how it was understood by the one who received it.

They asked again, but she had her family.

She later believed they were proposing a ceremony akin to marriage that would make her part of their family in everybody's heavenly afterward.

She heard them saying: We are yours as you are ours; live with us in heaven, too.

Some months later, Mr. Smith was gone, and she asked for the ceremony to be conducted by proxy.

But by then she was walking into the territory of Mr. Young.

Around 1845, when Mr. Smith was dead, Miss Manning married a Mr. James and was again with child.

In 1846 they crossed the river. Mrs. Sessions would deliver at least two of her seven children, Silas in 1846, Mary Ann in 1848.

Mrs. Sessions and Mrs. James traveled in the same company from Mount Pisgah, Iowa, to the Utah valley: two territories named for the peoples they crossed out.

Against a backdrop of displacements and changing rules of engagement, Mrs. James petitioned to accept the adoption Mr. Smith had promised.

She said in her plea: "He treated me as his own."

The words can sound like ownership or mutual belonging.

In the syntactical vibration between subject and object, I would like to think they belonged to each other in ways that were not replicated or replaced by other relationships.

Mr. Young repeatedly denied her petitions.

Had she been betrayed by one prophet or both?

It is unclear what position she would have held in the Smith family imaginary, but entirely clear how it was read by the family that replaced them.

When Mr. and Mrs. James arrived in the homeland of the Utes, they were employed in the service of Mr. Young who, a few years later, signed into law the "Act in Relation to Service," effectively legalizing indentured servitude and enabling any converts arriving with enslaved workers to continue to enslave them.

One prophet had been an abolitionist, the other claimed neutrality; that is, he stood with the slave owners.

Though Jane's legal status didn't change, her experience of relation and risk were radically altered.

In her appeal to Mr. Young, Mrs. James (by then Mrs. Perkins) was reported to have said "I am white with the exception of the color of my skin."

She may have been speaking in the racialized metaphors of US colonial English whereby whiteness was equated with an absence of sin.

She may have been thinking of an unstained book.

She may have been speaking of whiteness as a garment and race as a social construct that— by her own revelation and by means of basic logic—could be seen otherwise by anyone who took the trouble to see.

Ellen Madora was Mrs. James's fifth child. What does she have to say?

Her archival footprint is even smaller than her mother's.

In the 1870 census her occupation is "keeping house."

It is unclear if she kept her own house or another's or if it differed at all from the occupation of "keeping a house of ill fame," for which she was fined $50 in the 1870s by a San Francisco court.

At eighteen, she had a one-year-old, whose father's name is missing from the record.

It seems she eventually returned to the growing city by the inland sea, then left again for Wyoming, where Miss Ellen Madora James became Miss Nellie Kidd.

What circumstances were involved in her shift from girl to mother and from housekeeping to keeping house, from domestic virtue to ill repute, from one state or territory to another, we don't know.

What were her options.

Spirit was a way of understanding the god within the human, the human in nature, and nature's place among the gods: a spirit inhabits a body the way events can haunt a landscape, the way future and past involuntarily occupy the present.

In the visual language of the spirit, a body is a bird house. Still and small, a voice capable of anything.

A lark or nightingale or mockingbird. A prophet or liar or poet.

Or a woman among others, understood by sisters in the same field of enchantment.

Jane Elizabeth Manning & Jane James & Jane Elizabeth Perkins spoke in tongues in one body and were interpreted by and with others.

That is, they were transported by words from one world to another without having to go alone.

Sometimes words or touch can heal what ails you.

Why would she give that up to return to a world in which most folks seemed to think they knew everything she had to say?

It's a long way back to a place that no longer exists.

PEREGRINATIONS

orig. and chiefly *Theol.* The course of a person's life viewed originally as a temporary sojourn on earth (cf. sense 4b) and hence as a spiritual journey, esp. to heaven. Now *rare.* Cf. pilgrimage *n.* 1b.

Perrigrine Sessions was the most eccentric speller in a family of creative orthographers.

His peregrination began in Maine.

His mother, Mrs. Sessions, was delivered of him by her mother-in-law from whom she learned the art of midwifery.

At the age of twenty-one he was baptized by a Mr. Partridge, whose daughters Emily and Eliza were just older and younger than he was. As they, in the 1840s, became plural wives of Mr. Smith, he became the Prest.'s bodyguard.

Like his mother, Mr. Sessions kept a book of his life, devoted more to narrative facts and occasions of accounting than to his feelings about what he did or was done to him.

His diaries were published a century later under the title *Exemplary Elder*, which suspends the question of how he was exemplary.

A model to be emulated or a peculiar specimen in need of classification.

I first thought
I had a long journey to perform
but previous to my final departure
I had to go to a cirtin place
I then went and dressed my self
in the best I had

My Wife tied on my cravat
and comed my hare
and when she had done that
she kissed me and I went out
of my own house

as I traviled on I next found
my self in a strait roade
and a little riseing ground
with a green plaine before me
the grass looked [f]ine and
waved by the wind [*corner torn*]

At last I came to a Town
of eligant abuildings on the left
and on the rite hand side
there was barnes and shops
all doors were shet
and no one in the street

I [went] some half a Mile
to the end of the Street
whare I saw a door open
and a Yong Man
about twenty five years old
s[t]ood by my side
it seamed to be a Smith Shop

the smith was dresed in clean Clothes
and had a splendid shop and tools
there was some words [*corner torn*]
betwene us but I [*torn*]
forgoten them

[*torn*] band of Music and singing
that was splendid to here
the yong man said to me let us go
and I saw a large door open
whare the Musick came from

we went up too the door and I
rapt on the door Cheak and
a tall Woman came to the door
and hade us come inn
she had a brush and combs
in her hands and her hare
handing [hanging] down
and not comed as we entered

She shoed us a seat on a sophey
that was verry nice
and the Room seamed filled
with Wiming [women] and it [was as]
large and Splendid [as] I ever saw
thousands looking just like her
from infants to Old age
in diferents classes

here I saw my Mother
with many others of My neighbors
some that are dead
the whole Mass of people looked
in the vigar of life

not one sick or death like
all looked hapy here I gased [gazed]
upon the Multitudes and reflected
whare am I and who are all these

After a long reflection
a man commenced to talk
but in another language
I could not under stand
after talking awhile he stopt
and the musick began
and plaid and sung

Oh Susannah the music
almost charmed [*torn*]
[it was] so sweet
the speaker began to speak
in my own tung and
evry word filled me with joy

he said we will close and all
arose to their feet and he closed
by up lifted hands the people began
to come down from over head
and the yong man said let us [*torn*]

and as I stept out the door I awoke
and it seamed as tho it was a reality
for a long time after
I told my Wife the Dreem
and After some time
went to sleep againe
and saw the same things againe

and it seamed as tho
it was a reality and a recolection
that [I had] [s]een it before
thus the Dream closed but
my mind seamed to bee calm
as a summer s Morning

This dream I write
with my own hand
City Bountiful
August 21/1852
P.G Sessions

Mr. Sessions married Miss Bryson when he was fifty-two and she was sixteen.

She was his sixth wife.

She bore ten children, the sixth of whom was named Patty after Perrigrine's mother.

The second Patty's youth was set in a household of seven mothers and an absent father.

There must have been times when she felt anonymous, but I don't think she ever felt like a motherless child.

When she talked about her childhood, she said a family is a union full of different states of mind.

Dark secrets: facts a group conceals about itself *that are incompatible with the image it presents to its audience.*

Strategic secrets: used by *armies or businesses designing future actions.*

Possession of inside secrets *marks an individual as a member.*

Disclosure threatens the possessor of an entrusted secret.

Free secrets may be disclosed *without discrediting oneself.*

Secrecy creates members and outsiders.

Revelation turns belonging into law.

If you are a member, what do you belong to. You belong to us but you have to say so.

You have to turn your life into a book.

You have to make an effigy of your days.

When you write it down, you give it a body, and the body takes your name.

A letter may stand in for a name that can't be said or a face that can't be seen. A space to carry all its meaning in what isn't said.

Bound by syntax, a word may yet contain boundlessness.

Even *god* is a word.

A gap in the text to show how distance can tear anything apart.

Put a fence around this feeling. A story takes shape fitfully, in episodes.

The eye that sees you is larger than the sun.

Dear reader.

She's looking for a way between the words. To make of this chaos a forest, of the forest a house, and of this house a book.

If the word is law, is it a question or a statement.

It sneaks into the bedroom as the church climbs through the window.

A word is being written in a Book of Creation. A body taken by the thigh is given the name of a nation.

A word like *wife* or *marriage* will linger in a courtroom, its legislation sending you to hell or to heaven.

It will draw an imaginary line between domestic and civic worlds. It will build a fence around the meadow of an American dream.

A word like *brother* or *sister* can rearrange the world.

Everything can be translated into yes and no, darkness and light. Like Adam, every writer falls.

"Word" is saving a file called "To Be."

Raw. Infinitive. Query. A signal into space.

I want to survive. I want to outlast it.

There was a time when Mr. Sessions was coated with the tar and feathers intended for Mr. Smith.

Such an occurrence might be called by those in charge a "pillow party": a practice, like scalping, that had a long history in Europe.

When I see the tiny face of Mr. Sessions holding still for a camera, I think his suffering had meanings I can't discern, just as it involved sensations I haven't felt.

In the deep foreshortening of cultural memory, I wonder by what neural pathways such an event would strengthen a body's trust in a god rather than destroy its faith in mankind.

I think it affirmed his place within an expanding family structure.

He was quoted as saying it was the finest coat he ever wore.

The further in you are, the more you have lost, the harder it is to see what lives outside it, and to see that outside as anything but a threat.

I think of the woman who took it off and how.

I think: from inside the well-lit circle of a central fire, the dark beyond might feel enveloping or uniformly blank.

I think: these people mostly seemed to pass safely from one state into another.

I think: he was lucky not to have been set on fire.

Smith & Young
in the trees' dark
lace

necessity calling
on the young
smith

old young
lobbing
for his coat

The family business
projected
into heaven

A mirror
a reproductive
organ

How did it feel
taking what it
took

from the expanding
buffet
more than one Eliza

on a dare
Augusta, already
Mrs. Cobb

What did she miss
in his picture
of the future

The abandonment
of children
is one test

of allegiance
as the known world
expires

into the urgency
of a petition
to one man

or another
on behalf
of a young son

for whom
the lord may speak
as a mother

The tapping out
of a game
will shorten

a day of travel
by giving it
a rhythm

a hinge
to the other life
even

as the evening
stitches everything
into place

old young
pulling closed
the curtain

young smith
in his
blast of light

falling from
that height
like an idol

shaking like the star
that knows its fate
within the field, across the line

MISS ADAMS, MRS. COBB & MRS. YOUNG;
OR,
THE ANGEL OF THE CHURCH AT SALT LAKE;
HER ALIEN, HER PROXY

I felt like a caged lioness.

Elizabeth Cady Stanton

Lions roar with glorious precision.

Robert Walser

When his new city was finally constructed, Mr. Young resided in the Lion House and worked next door in the Beehive House. Or was it the other way round.

Both buildings rested at the intersection of Temple and State streets, in the precise center of the map.

The relation between his bedroom and the territorial headquarters was the relation between the lion and the bee.

In this intemperate adaptation of Samson's riddle, the body of the lion formed the borders of a state that thought of itself as a beehive.

In its stylized form, the state emblem looks like a heap of rope waiting for a pulley.

Drawn by popular accounts of Mormon harems, Richard F. Burton, the sexual adventurer and translator of the *Arabian Nights*, visited the Great Salt Lake settlement in 1860.

He admired Brigham Young's many-gabled house. He looked for the company of women.

Traveling through the Middle East in disguise, Mr. Burton had become a professional connoisseur of the hidden.

He wanted to get inside the temple but had to rely on the words of local informants whose accounts of its rituals focused on a theatrical event which Burton likened to a mystery play or divine comedy: "possibly Paradise Lost and Paradise Regained."

In the middle of a building in the middle of a desert, an imaginary garden with real people re-enacts a scene of first encounter.

There is no escaping the arc of the story.

There is no way out once you've walked through its door. Except for the door that leads to empty space.

To survive, you have to stay in the supply chain, to accept the movement from garden to exile. You must become a vessel in a world of proxies. A proxy in the great narrative chain.

Then a shining city in the heavens can be yours.

In 1802 Augusta Adams was born to John Adams and Mary Ives of Lynn, Massachusetts.

At a proper age she met Mr. James Cobb of Boston and bore eight children, seven of whom survived.

After hearing the gospel according to Mr. Young, she ran away with same under cover of night, bringing only her infant.

They married for "time" while she remained married to Mr. Cobb, who eventually filed for divorce.

Mrs. Cobb's feelings about Mr. Young varied widely.

She defended him fiercely, professing both devotion and disdain.

She prophesied to the prophet on the subject of his own hypocrisy, assuring him that his errors in judgment would be met with appropriate retribution.

She called herself the lioness of the lord.

That is, her revelations sometimes came in the form of poems or letters that served to correct the legally binding pronouncements of Mr. Young in the lion's house.

March 24, 1852

Mr Pilate, Just as I was getting on briskly all at once my little
Bark came to a dead stand, and now I ask what I must do next?

[…]

By the way there is a huge brass kettel directly across my path at
present time what is to be done

[…]

Now Brigham its you and I again force [illegible] feel the Spirit
comeing on and Wo wo if you do not listen. For I fear that things
are aproximating to a fearfull Cricis with you and me. And what
the end will be God knows force do not. But one thing I do
know for certain and that is I have got to have more liberty and
more enlargement I have had to contend with the Devel and his
imps inch by inch thus far and stand in the defensive alone I am
completely tired of it. You are upheld by Heber and many of your
Brethren while I am persecuted on every side. And all manner
of evil said about me. The Ancients when they were persecuted
In one City fled to another, But I have to live under the lash
continually. There is only one poor solitary being that I have dare
open my whole heart to, and that is Emily who is much in the
same Condition. Well May the Lord bless her for her patience and
labour of love I would like to see you this evening if convenient
for I have somewhat against the. Thus saith the Spirit to the
Angel of the Church at Salt Lake

*

Friday noon
June 11th 1852

My Dear Alien,
… it is so long since I have addressed you that I have almost
forgotten what to call you …
[…]

I do not feel good at all towards you and I want you to know it.…
   Alieness.—

                              *

June 17, 1852

Br Brigham you have probably learned that ere this the same
hand that wounds can also heal, If you have not I have And if I
have made you sorry who is he that maketh me glad but the same
which is made sory by me. There is diversities of gifts but the
same Spiret, and there are differences of Administrations but the
Same Lord And there are diversities of apparitions but it is the
same God which worketh all in all. Now you must be satisfied
that one of the gifts of God to me is writing I take no praise to my
self I give the glory to him For I know by useing and improveing
upon this gift it has been a means of not only prolonging my life
but actually Saveing it For Brigham I never could have talked the
things I have written to you no never, Therefore my mind would
have become darkened and over charged consequently my faith
would have been weak and where faith is weak persons will not
be able to contend against all the opposition, tribulation and
afflictions they will have to encounter in order to be heirs of God.
[…] I feel again as If I could run through a troop or leap a wall,
why because I have freed my mind again to you.

                              *

To President B. Young February 14, 1853

A dungeon this world has become to me

[...]

and I am desolate and forlorn

[...]

Not so with my Proxy; he's gay as a lark

[...]

PROPHET
PRESIDENT
GOVERNOR
PILATE
ALIEN
PROXY

Mrs. Young's daughter Miss Charlotte Ives Cobb first married a Mr. William Godbe just as he became the leader of the dissident, liberal Godbeites who formed the Church of Zion.

The Godbes invited and hosted Mrs. E. C. Stanton and Mrs. S. B. Anthony in Great Salt Lake City in 1871.

Eventually Mr. and Mrs. Godbe divorced, and Mrs. Godbe devoted her time to women's suffrage and remarried a mine-owning Mr. Kirby who didn't like church at all.

When Augusta Adams Cobb Young died, she was buried beside Mr. Young and his first wife Mary Ann in their family plot.

But a few years later Mrs. Charlotte Cobb Godbe Kirby had her mother pulled out and replanted in the plot next to her own.

THE ADAMS FAMILY

Asenath Annie Adams grew up in a log house with three mothers and a father.

When the father died, the three mothers lived on, down Little Cottonwood Canyon.

The girl, this Annie, could throw her voice to the back of a room and up the side of a mountain.

A few nights a week she put on a hat or an apron or a scarf and mounted a platform to practice the martial art of public emotion.

She stood beside herself in the oily light and said someone else's words.

She said them in tents and living rooms and dance halls, on makeshift stages placed on scaffolds.

When she was old enough to travel to the city on her own, Asenath Annie joined one of the earliest troupes of actors on the stage of the Salt Lake City Theatre, beneath a bust of Mr. Young.

Sometimes she traveled with other actors to San Francisco and Reno.

When she married it was to a man from elsewhere. A man with a different story.

Some said the husband had been a banker. Some said, No, he was a Banker, nice Ohio family.

Was it her husband or her father whose past had drawn a crooked line through Canada?

Was he wanted or wanting, a criminal or a prospector?

He was Kiskaden or Kiskadden, a name that rattled in the mouth, mumbling out a story that could be changed to suit the speaker.

No one expected him to go to church.

Soon there was a daughter. Then there was no husband. No one talked about where he went or how he died. There was Virginia City where he liked to gamble. San Francisco where he lost his shirt.

Somewhere along the line A. A. Adams bore a close resemblance to a Mrs. Harvey Glidden.

Somewhere else she encountered Arthur Brown, a Republican senator whose mistress shot him when she found the scented letters of a certain actress who went by the initials A. A. A.

Her carte de visite shows her wearing a large hat and a wry smile. She has signed it *Faithfully*.

The daughter of Asenath Annie was Maudie, then Maude. She
was Kiskadden, then Adams.

An errant thread leading back to Boston tugged to the surface.

The girl was said to be related, at a distance, to two presidents. No
one could say her father's name for sure.

Maudie seemed to be in Annie's arms whenever Annie wasn't
moving right or left across the stage of the Salt Lake City Theatre.

Her cradle was placed beyond the unused painted backdrops
past the second curtain, between "The Iron Horse" and "The
Return of the Fleet," where she could hear voices swinging out
and bouncing back, where a minor character could reach out a
slippered foot and rock her to sleep.

There was a boy baby in the theater who wouldn't stop crying. An acting baby at the center of a play. *The Lost Child* was a farce about a broken family, in which all would be restored.

Little Maude Adams was backstage with her mother between scenes. The stage manager sent the crying baby home and snatched Maudie from her cradle. He "thrust" her onto a platter and she entered the story's dining room like a tiny John the Baptist.

No, not like a wild-bearded disciple. Like Isaac being led by a parent into a sacrificial wilderness of empty plates and imaginary food.

Maude was nine months old when she replaced the howling two-month-old boy. The audience cheered at the baby's superhuman growth between Acts two and three.

Maude Adams had entered the region of performance. The accident of an art in love with accident. In a city in love with young girls.

Light had snagged her organdy dress. The future was coming on. Like the croup. Like the morning.

When you have the power to become someone else in the heat of a blinding light, anything can seem normal.

Maude found her place in Zion as a surrogate. She became the boy baby pretending to be another baby in a fiction unfolding on the elevated shore of a dark-faced sea.

She could look back at the invisible rustling monsters of the deep and say the magic words. She could pretend the only eyes in the room were her eyes looking out at the unknown.

On stage, Asenath Annie Adams flashes before her child like a deity, a flame too blue to see. She's composed of that instant, a mother in heaven, exhausted by the bright air.

She can see everything while Maude can see nothing. She's made a mess of the bed, of the stage. She's been doubled, she's survived.

So Maude Adams emerged from the Theatre's long dark wings headfirst into the slippery hands of a theocratic world that already considered itself a stage. A city built on a bright desert platform, the platform set against a painted backdrop, jagged mountains layered on an icy sky.

A revelation, an apocalypse, the blue sublime.

The Theatre was the finest building in G. S. L. City. It was rushed into being, with no expense spared, and dedicated in 1862, thirty-one years before the completion of the city's temple.

In place of the masks traditionally carved above the stage, a semblance of Mr. Young surveyed the audience: comedy and tragedy in one.

On this stage a new idea of the family was being performed, a new idea of the state was being assayed.

It was meant to be paradise. With clothes.

In a frontier theater, pine is painted to look like Eastern oak or Italian marble.

A velvet drape smudges the boundary between what you're meant to see and what you're not.

A theater is sacred. It has its own rules.

A temple is a theater. A portal for enchantments.

Someone builds the machinery whereby a god shapes the arc of events from behind a curtain. A god with three names and more than one person to love. A god who could make a girl pregnant with a glance, the brush of a wing against her belly.

Little Maude Adams would fly from that performance to the neverland of the Eastern theater.

She would refuse to remain on the eternal platter; she would stand up, she would run, she would take a train. She would become other people with other addresses.

A woman. A man. A boy.

In her eastern hereafter, Maude Adams would grow younger and younger.

As a girl she played a crone. As a woman she became a handsome young officer.

Briefly Napoleon. For a time, Joan of Arc. Definitively, Peter Pan.

It was said J. M. Barrie had seen in her a real boy on an imaginary island. A boy clothed in leaves, pleased with his costume, with the brightness on his skin.

It was reported that Maude Adams considered herself a foundling and that she had no thoughts of young men or of marriage. It was said that, like her mother, she had married the theater.

In fact, she made enough money to live in three different houses with two other women.

On Broadway and at home, Napoleon and Joan of Arc and Peter Pan liked the sensation of closing the curtain or the door; of changing the setting, the role, the gender, the age.

This Maude who liked to say the words written down by others liked to have her own words written down by a secretary.

Naturally she liked the secretary to be in the same house. Naturally such a secretary would be a woman whose voice she preferred above all others.

She liked the sound of her secretary's name, and she liked saying it in a certain way that would mean "Come."

The secretary, Louise Boynton, too had no thoughts of marriage unless it were the thought of being married to someone who was married to the theater.

Asenath Annie Adams joined them to live again among women in an unmanned house.

If a theater is a house, is a house a theater?

Maude wrote: *Genius is the talent for seeing things straight. It is seeing things in a straight line without any bend or break or aberration of sight, seeing them as they are, without any warping of vision. Flawless mental sight.*

How queerly can you see clearly? Was seeing straight a role, a costume, a cover?

Or did it mean creating a world beside itself, from which you could see clearly? How queerly can you see straight?

A peasant blouse falls open to a shoulder, the bodice so loose it appears to be mistied. The advertisement by Alphonse Mucha isn't a statement but a set of questions. A portrait in fragments.

Has she just endured or is she heading toward an assault or a revelation?

This girl. This peasant. This face that breaks the field of the beaux-arts world that swirls around it.

She has learned to speak without a voice, to act, as Ellen Terry put it, from the corners of her eyes.

The flowering stump in the foreground snags, then reflects, the gesture of Maude's upraised hand, the open vulnerability of the face, the delicacy of something fine, unarmored.

The torn pink shawl suggests an earthly shell, the emblem of a body on its doomed way to sainthood.

Her hands are raised in an attitude of listening. You can close your eyes but not your ears.

You can see that listening has a special relationship with pain.

The girl is trying to take it in, trying to hear something small behind the noise. Or she is trying to shake off the entire scene.

To refuse to be an object. *She* is not *the.*

Saint Joan's accusers referred to her as The Maid. An epithet carried like a weapon. To be the servant of a god is to be both more and less than human.

This is her mantle, her future. The cry of her occasion.

No man knows another, and every man is ever another to himself. The epigraph to Maude's autobiography comes from *The Adventures of François: Foundling, Thief, Juggler, and Fencing-Master During the French Revolution.*

François is a lost boy caught between fiction and nonfiction. What had Maude in common with foundlings, fencing-masters, jugglers, or thieves?

It is said that in the performance of family, everyone must share a community of fate or be cast forever into an outer dark.

The future of Maude's childhood was full of astronauts: men and women inhabiting new planets, and the unlucky few whose cord had been severed, who could only drift into the cold black space above the mountains.

In *Peter Pan*, Maude oversees a dominion made entirely of children, an alternative domestic arrangement of resemblance, affinities, and love.

What is the boy's message?

Believe and you will have power over life and death. Believe and you can save your friends.

In the world outside the play, Maude's performance would attract a nation's worth of lost children and adults—including one night in 1909, the entire population of the Mormon Tabernacle Choir— to a dream they could barely remember the next morning.

They would watch their lives unfold like a leaf in an allegory on a stage. They could think of the sky as inhabited by children who had no other way to escape, so they jumped.

A play about the delicate webs of freedom and imagination would make its star the highest-paid woman in the theater. Maude would be caught in it for the rest of her life.

In her favorite publicity shot from *Peter Pan*, Maude appears stage center with her arms flung wide, fencing with Captain Hook. It's a gesture of righteous abandon.

The lost boys are behind her, looking lost.

Maude is dressed in knickers and boots and a big white shirt. The captain wears elevator shoes and a coat that fits like a little black dress.

The girl in pants is thinking of Joan of Arc. In her heart she's a girl saving France, loved by her troops. She's on a horse. She's more popular than the pope.

She has put the king of the world's sexiest country back on his sexy little stage.

Before she is burned at the stake, she is placed in a room in a tower. It smells like a stable.

One night, like Peter Pan, she leaps from the window. Or rather, *he* jumps like *her*.

She said she preferred her flag to her sword.

No one was sure what year she was born.

THE WRITING ON THE WALL

The more I smelled the lion, the more loudly I sang.

Leonora Carrington

Some consider Hercules the first liontamer, though strictly speaking his labors involved killing a lion, not training one. He's usually seen wearing a lion's skin and carrying a club.

Others point to Daniel, a previously unremarkable prince who lived among lions only briefly.

Daniel's people had "fallen" into bondage, and Daniel was the kind of person worth capturing. That's how he got the attention of the conquering Babylonian king. He had a talent for finding an audience without getting killed.

When Nebuchadnezzar had a dream, Daniel could see it projected on a wall: a screen full of bubble letters tagged by a gigantic hand.

When he told the king what he didn't want to hear, it only made the king trust him more.

But jealous courtiers threw him in a house of lions where he had to choose between an impossible struggle to the death and the ridiculous appearance of refusing to fight at all.

And that's what he did, waited it out like the rest of them, thinking about his next meal.

In one account, he's saved by an angel who has taken the appearance of a lion so as to fend off his adversaries. In this case, it is essentially a mirror that saves his life—one wild face staring down another.

Three of Daniel's smartest, wealthiest, best-looking friends were taken with him into bondage and given Babylonian names that held them together like an iron chain.

They had never met the king and wouldn't bow down to an image whose power they didn't believe in.

For thinking they had a choice, they were placed inside an oven, a pattern repeated throughout children's literature.

Shadrach, Meshach, and Abednego, it was said, walked into the fire and came straight out the other side, like lions strolling through a hoop.

Because they didn't believe a king had the authority to destroy them, their names entered history.

No, not everyone who refuses to bow down is able to walk away. Tragedy doesn't improve those who survive it any more than a fire can cleanse everything it touches.

The refiner's fire either devours or illuminates with a light beyond light, a law beyond law.

The man of straw will disappear. The man of clay will shatter. The man of steel will melt. We don't know what to call the substance of the thing that survives.

The point of the fable is not that friendship will keep you safe but that your gods, singular or plural, will have your back if you bow down only to them.

Still, the gods say, we reserve the right to bat you around until you become a thing whose fate we'll make a joke of deciding.

The unpredictability of gods and their insistence that there is no higher body to which you can appeal: This is what makes religion a captivity narrative.

The biggest cats are defined not by their size but their sound. Like Joshua's horn, they make previous understandings of safety dissolve into a wave that is felt as much as heard.

Such is their power that a lion lounging with a lamb is the paragon of post-apocalyptic equipoise.

If lions didn't sound like proof of natural dominion, they wouldn't so fully inhabit the language of power.

When I feel them shake the air, what do I not understand?

Tertullian considered Circe the master of the first circus. Therefore the word bears, or bends, her name.

Her villa was surrounded by wild creatures who, in her presence, wandered around like pets. She lived on an island made entirely of vowels.

From offshore it sounded more like a moan than a cry.

Circe's clock spun on an axis of natural rather than military power.

Some say she tricked Odysseus into forgetting about his wife and dog, but it was he who chose to spend the year with her a few hours from his unraveling home.

A concentrated gaze can dull the minds of would-be conquerors.

Seen from this distance, Circe resembles Penelope, whose hand she has taken to dwell with other artists making worlds of their resistance in the fields between the humans and the gods.

Nature has a material magic whereby everything that has come apart is recombined.

Where Circe walks, her lovers walk
               When they walk, they move in circles
past the same bodega
          the same stand of trees   the same unexpected cove
At each revolution
         they come closer to their own mystery
                    just as their lover
remains the factual geography
          around which they turn
                  Some call this
tyranny
    but who among them would not choose
           to make a science of her breath
with one leg on a trapeze
        and a cheek brushing the grass
            In one of Dosso Dossi's portraits
Circe's lovers graze among fritillary trees
          on a tiny rise
            above a pale jagged creek
We know she is their teacher
       because in the visual language
            of 17th-century Italy
she gestures toward a stone tablet
         This is their frontier
She is free to teach naked
      this bunch of sailors
        That's how much they have to learn
The hands that have stroked and fed them
         touch words with an unfamiliar
tenderness to show them
      something else about desire
         Dossi is known
for sprezzatura
   a "studied carelessness" of style
        but also often of subject

so we see in Circe
                              the relaxed precision
          of an artist saying something
                                        otherwise unrecognizable
to the world of rigging and levers and wars
                                        She is their Futurist
                                                  replacing
their cargo with a cosmos
                              whose polymorphous abundance
lies outside history

A circus wants to be a temporary universe expanding and contracting in the fields around medium-sized towns.

Histories of failure breathe through the animal closeness of its giant canvas mouth.

The performer's condition is sacrificial, calculated: the gasp, the leap, the dare.

Dear reader of her wildly looping letters, it is among others that you approach the sympathies of her world. Your chalked feet planted on the back of a horse, your nerves lit up with risk.

Every trick within the ring is exactly what it appears to be; not a trick at all but a *spectacle of actuality* surrounded by witnesses.

The knife thrower, the acrobat, the tamer of large cats surrounded by a watchful sea.

Audacity can move you from one place to another. New neighborhood, new clothes, new friends.

You can summon voices. When it works, you feel the touch of electricity. A rigorous disobedience ready to tear you apart.

A leap at the site of magic or faith depends on the resilience of everyday belief structures: today will resemble yesterday, therefore its disruption is miraculous.

Churches try to file a patent on this magic: to monopolize, to gender, to weaponize it. To place it before you, above and up ahead.

At the end of the road, behind the curtain, in its jewel-like architectures.

George Wombwell was born in England after his empire's American plantations had traded one kind of debt for another.

He fell in love with making things from the skins of animals and apprenticed to a cobbler.

He started buying exotic creatures off the London docks—boa constrictors, an elephant, an ostrich, a leopard—and displaying them in taverns for a fee.

In 1810, Wombwell's menagerie started touring the countryside, and by 1839, you could smell the caravan a few hours away.

Newly chained animals were given free tours of England though some were taxed to death by the inhospitality of the climate, a loss he could sometimes recuperate with the help of a taxidermist.

An aegis is a shield of animal skin offering spiritual or physical protection. The word now refers largely to organizations that purport to protect their members even if they exercise their power to obliterate them.

His show was technically more of a parade than a circus. Its spectators streamed past, captivated by their view of captivity.

Mr. Wombwell's animals included William, the first lion bred in British captivity. He referred to his rhinoceros as a unicorn.

He was summoned three times by Victoria Regina, a large queen at the center of an enormous global hive. A woman who abhorred slavery just enough to move it offshore. Who placed herself atop a great chain of being and never refused a parade.

When you bow to a queen, you must move like a pawn, approaching and retreating in a straight line without turning your back.

Mr. Wombwell appeared offstage in a story by Arthur Conan Doyle. He cured Prince Albert's dogs and was given, in payment, a cartload of wood salvaged from the HMS *Royal George*, from which he fashioned his own coffin.

Eventually George Wombwell, born into the working class, would become one with the remains of that other George that had touched eternal life as it was overloaded with rum headed back to the colonies.

Mr. Wombwell commissioned a replica of his favorite lion, Nero, to be installed in stone a few feet above his grave.

When Nero spoke, he raged against captivity with an eloquence beyond mastery. He longed for the one who had enchanted and lain with him and understood everything he said.

When it comes to lions, taming would more accurately be called training. Lions understand the location of their dinner and how to claim it.

If their contract lapses or their tolerance for boredom and cheap meat finds an end, they will on occasion turn to the nearest mammal. Or they will die of sadness.

Early trainers like Mr. Wombwell beat their animals into submission and baited them with packs of dogs.

Isaac Van Amburgh, an American who toured Europe, trained his lions using a crowbar. He was beloved of Queen Victoria, who liked to see his entire head safely retracted from a lion's open mouth.

He was often referred to as the Lion King, a cruel aristocrat whose subjects were trained to tolerate a bondage they seldom outlasted.

When he ordered his lions to bow down, they did so. When he set a hoop on fire, they leapt through.

Sir Edwin Henry Landseer's painting of Isaac van Amburgh lives in the Windsors' royal collection of art. In it, Mr. Van Amburgh reclines in a large cage with a lion at his back, a lamb on his lap, and his right hand stroking the head of a tiger. The man is out of time in a medieval coat of mail and the ancient sandals of a Roman centurion.

As viewers, we occupy the cage with this man and the other animals; the Victorian spectators strolling past the cage are pictured behind bars.

Like the royal viewers to whom the painting belongs, we are citizens of a darkened parlor of human dominion and colonial power, held in a delicate equilibrium by a crowbar stowed in the folds of a sweaty woolen cape.

Clyde Beatty, star of *The Big Cage* (1933), is said to be the first person to train his lions with a chair.

A lion may be tamed by a chair not because it's afraid of being beaten but because it is confounded by the need to address all four legs at once.

As a broom becomes a witch, so a chair becomes a liontamer. The most powerful acts of enchantment accomplished by the simplest of domestic tools. Objects so commonplace, they are practically invisible.

The audience, not the lion, is tamed with the whip, as it controls the process by which one is hypnotized and awakened. The big cage is the one you're in, not the one you're watching.

It says: one day you too may find yourself looking at the legs of a chair, longing for Circe, remembering what it was like to run.

The rush every night of surviving flight. A butterfly dance, a girl in the air.

In 1917, her fall is specific. Not like Eve but like a girl on a horse in a show. And when someone spooks the horse, it all comes down.

There's fire all around them running through the animal hay.

The whole town's been on fire including the hospital, so she's taken to the minister's house where she'll compete for his love with every woman in town.

In this version Polly's just a girl with two men as her mothers. A year later she's declaring her love for a preacher twice her age. Suddenly she's the multitude on the man's crowded hill.

In 1932 she's all dance and bravado on the brushed aluminum train, eating someone else's sandwich, drinking their coffee, taking what she wants.

She's an innocent with a mouth on her, entering another ring of performance where the crowd can't be charmed.

She calls her man "the sky pilot of this burg." He's a "gospel slinger" selling the same old book.

The pre-code petulance of Marion Davies: this lush flower swinging in a basket, suddenly bruised by his critique.

How will she be judged. How will she survive. How will she choose to live through the night.

The churchman's an orphan like her, a boy in the gym among boys. She'll fall for his dark lashes any way the script allows.

Onscreen, the circus looks like the antipode of the church.

But in its basic fugitivity, the circus family is stronger than the straight one presumed to exist in the offstage church; it's bound by its commitment to risk, the inevitability of disaster.

So it's Polly who converts him; he who sets aside childish things to find another way to read.

It's the story of Ruth that brings them together, two women on the brink with a new way of defining trust. She's Polly, he's Bible. All families are eventually a little queer.

The spirit is holy because it leaps through everyone.

MR. ROBERTS

And now I'm in the world alone,
Upon the wide, wide sea

Lord Byron, *Childe Harold's Pilgrimage*

Henry Roberts was born in Lancashire in 1857 to a seamstress who couldn't forgive him for the trouble he caused her.

He arrived too late for the Crystal Palace. Revolutions had come and gone.

She started staying out late to hear a man in the park talking up a new book.

One day a crew came by to pick her up and dip her in the Irish Sea.

Henry's father too was dipped but kept up his profession as a drunken, cheating gambler. When the law was after him, he proved his helplessness by beating a small boy.

When Henry's sister was born, the father disappeared. When the father disappeared, the seamstress started carrying a rope in the pocket of her coat.

She was hanging on to a thread pulled out and away through the eye of a needle too big to see.

The boy never quite had a family or they were never in the same room.

His mother stepped onto a packet boat, looking for a life with the Mormons sailing out of Liverpool. Her boy was five: old enough to be sold or leased or left behind, old enough to earn a living and pay his own way.

There was a market for youth; there were futures on Henry that could be leveraged for a new start in a new territory beyond the queen and the president and the united states of anything.

Henry was taken home by a Mr. and Mrs. Tovey, previously the Gailies, which was not their name either. The Toveys appeared to be converts too, just trying to help a family in distress.

Even as a boy locked in the Toveys' cupboard, Henry admired his mother's instinct for self-preservation.

He ran away twice. He walked across England in both directions, looking for a way out.

The boy began to know that he lived on an island. His biographer calls him a young Crusoe.

He could see he was a child-machine fed less fuel than it burned and if he continued to be a good boy he would die.

He was separated from his sister and found her again.

Henry sometimes went by Harry and when he could read, he fell in love with Childe Harold. He was headed for a dark tower. He was born at the bottom and would read his way up.

When his mother left him on the island so she could join the saints, she gave Henry the name Brigham, and when Harry was old enough to hold a knife he cut off all the letters but the ones that quietly pushed him forward through the sooty air. He became B. H.

Henry—sometimes Harry, later B. H.—described himself as gloomy and accustomed to being alone. He wore barn-door trousers and a jacket sewn from a policeman's coat.

He thought about his appearance but had little access to mirrors. Restless, ill-shaped, neither tender nor sweet. His head hunched into his shoulders; his teeth gapped. His purpose was invisible to everyone but himself.

When he thought of Lord Byron, he thought about his foot. Little Mr. Roberts could be brought to tears by the words of a drug-addled aristocrat printed in a book.

Harry made the six-week passage from Liverpool to New York in 1866 on the *John Bright* of the Union Line with nine hundred other commoners: servants, miners, chimney sweeps, factory workers, laundresses, bakers, and odd jobbers.

In the ship's log Henry is listed as age fifteen though he was barely ten. His sister is listed as age seventeen, occupation Spinster. The deposit on her passage is listed as £9/4s. "W.O. by Prest. Young." Some believers or their children were offered passage with a loan they could pay back in labor when they reached Utah Territory.

A few years earlier, when Charles Dickens boarded an emigrant ship to see what the fuss was about, there were fewer Mormons in Utah than in England.

It was not their unruly hair or misshapenness that struck Mr. Dickens about the passengers but their orderly movements: *They had not been a couple of hours on board when they established their own police.*

The ship, he said, was *as orderly and as quiet as a man of war.* To his eyes, they appeared to be *the pick and flower of England*, full of beauty and strength and the *capacity for work.*

Harry, indebted for his place on the crowded boat, finally stood on a new shore looking back at the island he had left.

His mouth was moving. He was making a sound like a trumpet. Words were taking him farther and farther from his father.

He identified with real and imaginary orphans.

Like St. Augustine, he wanted to return to the woman who had left him to be used by others but somehow also lived inside him. A word of betrayal leaves no mark against the skin.

When Henry crossed the ununited American interior, he did it on foot. Some of it without shoes. Some of it, he said, without clothes.

His travel took him through Carthage, or Carthage passed through him. He landed in the settlement established by Mrs. Sessions's son.

Eventually he would marry three women, the last of them a Dr. Shipp, several years his senior.

He would serve time in the Pen. He'd argue with the law in the house of power.

When he lost one battle, he would take on another.

He believed what was true could eventually be proven.

He believed the Book of Mormon could be adapted for the stage.

Before there were drones, there was chiseled stone and melted lead.

Before there were men on bicycles, there were men in rumpled jackets, sleeping under bridges in the rain.

Before there were nametags, there were handshakes and letters of introduction.

Behold the young Mr. Roberts, walking around Iowa and Tennessee with a book, just as he'd been told.

When he was lucky, someone fed him for a week just to hear him talk.

Young Mr. Roberts had trained as a blacksmith, but he preferred the clothing of a representative.

He liked the idea of changing someone's mind. He liked having more than one woman in his life.

He wanted to create a family who would not leave him in a cupboard on an island. He wanted to belong to more than one kind of house.

Mr. Roberts felt betrayed when polygamy was abandoned as a practice in exchange for Utah statehood. He believed there was no difference between revelation and fact. He didn't think the truth should change.

After serving time for cohabitation, Mr. Roberts was elected to the US Congress on the strength of the non-Mormon vote.

He moved to the capital to hear two years of debate on whether or not he would be allowed to sit with the other men at their boy-sized desks. He was not.

The men in the House of desks sent him back to the land of the Utes.

The church that liked to keep Mr. Roberts busy put him to work on a comprehensive account of its own history.

As his ardor became more difficult to manage, even for his brothers in the house of the Lord, he was sent East again, this time to Brooklyn to train young missionaries in the arts of persuasion.

Believing in proof would take some men toward integrated systems of thought and others toward the complex hierarchies of classification that buttressed the fields of phrenology and eugenics.

If you thought you stood at the top of a great chain and if the chain had given you a voice rather than taken it away, you might decide to make it as immutable as possible.

But even a great chain is a chain.

Mr. Theodore Schroeder, Esq., of Racine, Wisconsin; of Great Salt Lake City; and of Manhattan; believed in the legislation of the voice. After beginning his law career in Utah, he moved to Manhattan where he co-founded the Free Speech League, where he worked with Emma Goldman and Margaret Sanger.

At first Mr. Schroeder defended Mormonism, but the longer he lived in the Great Salt Lake City, the more he devoted his spare time to its critique.

He took many pseudonyms, some containing clues, puns, or inside jokes. He was at times Mr. Curtis or Mr. Heist of the *Salt Lake Tribune* and of *Lucifer's Lantern*.

He began collecting Augusta Adams Cobb Young's letters and prophecies regarding Mr. Young, along with writings by early converts who had decided to leave the church.

He called himself an evolutionary psychologist.

He argued that judges and teachers should be psychoanalyzed in order to free them from prejudice.

He proposed a multi-volume set entitled *My Criminal Friends* and legislated for statues of Thomas Paine to be installed in New York public schools.

His articles included

"Mental Hygiene for Non-combatants"
"Government by Spies"
"How Not to Teach Sex Hygiene"
"Witchcraft and Obscenity"
"The First US Fascist Dictatorship"
"Chattel and Wage Slavery"
"Concerning Free Love"

He was as captivated as Mr. Roberts by the intersection of proof and belief. When Mr. Roberts was elected to the House, it was Mr. Schroeder who prepared the case against him.

Their debate continued in and out of the pages of *American Historical Quarterly*.

Among Mr. Schroeder's boxes of correspondence is a fragment of a typed carbon addressed to "My Dear B. H.," which recounts a visit to *a queer little religious sect who heal by prayer and the laying on of hands* in the heart of Jersey City. It was a community largely of women who called each other Sister.

The letter is incomplete. Its writer may or may not have been Mr. Schroeder. Its recipient may or may not have been Mr. Roberts.

Hyrum Bischoff could freehand a billboard and walk on his hands.

In 1913 his father had launched the Armada, the first motion picture house in northern Wyoming and the first source of electricity in the Big Horn Basin.

After the last show, the seats and piano were pushed aside for roller skating.

Young Mr. Bischoff was responsible for agitprop and advertising. He'd paint signs in the morning and parade down Main Street wearing sandwich boards in the afternoon.

Eventually his church sent him to Brooklyn as a fisher of city dwellers. He stopped in Salt Lake City to be ordained, then walked a few blocks to the Empress Theatre to see Pola Negri in *Shadows of Paris*.

When he arrived in New York, he soapboxed in Union Square and chalked the sidewalks of Greenwich Village.

He found fantastic deals on straw hats, bought furs that he sent back to Wyoming for his mother and his girlfriend, and learned to play the sax.

He became the top Book of Mormon salesman on the Eastern seaboard.

He was a regular at Coney Island and the Broadway strip. On rainy days he made candy. He liked *Scaramouche* and the *Hunchback of Notre Dame* and the Ziegfeld Follies.

He had finally arrived in the heavenly city where gods in lamé gowns and designer suits were projected with a hot silver light onto the proscenium screen of converted vaudeville stages.

The Capital of Temptation was his City of God.

He thereby entered the Eastern States Mission under the jurisdiction of the aging Mr. Roberts, the most eccentric, zealous, and contradictory public figure in the church he had come to represent.

Mr. Roberts believed the translated text they were selling was of indigenous origin, the New World's link between Jerusalem and native America just as Mr. Smith had said it was.

If the story was true, there must be evidence.

He liked the confidence of his champion salesman. Together they decided to make a film.

What would be more convincing of an ancient golden book than the archaeological wonders of Central and South America, a visual record that would whiten up the world of pre-Columbian grandeur?

Mr. Bischoff collected film stock from studios in Manhattan and New Jersey, assembling retired documentary footage of Aztec ruins.

He consulted professors on their theories of lost tribes.

He took his flickering assemblage through the East, camping in fields and projecting images onto a bright white sheet hanging from the roof of his Model T.

Film is repetition with a difference. A utopian nowhere, everywhere at once. In it a body can be captivated by an act of witness.

In it anyone can live again and again.

First Book of Mormon Motion Picture Lecture

Otto Preminger's film based on Allen Drury's novel revolves around Mr. Anderson, a newly elected senator from Utah.

The man likes being at the beginning of the alphabet. He likes the new job. He likes his proximity to the god-like utterances of Law.

Like Mr. Roberts, he's married to a woman but has other alliances made in secret that, if made public, would expel him from the beltway of powerful men and spit him out among the asteroids.

Mr. Anderson shares Mr. Roberts's first name, which also belonged to the first governor of Utah whose Lion House rested at the corner of church and state.

His co-stars call him "Brig," which also means a seafaring jail. That's the kind of line he walks between appearance and fact.

Like Walt Whitman, he feels the pull of the capitol as if he were a renegade planet clinging to a wobbly astrolabe.

The capitol's design, including the woman soldier at the top of the outer dome, was overseen by US secretary of war Jefferson Davis before he became president of a different union.

"Armed Liberty" is many things at once: a woman holding a sword and wearing a helmet with the head of an eagle and a feathered crest *suggested by the costume of our Indian tribes*.

The senator wanders through the city looking for signs of understanding in the faces of other men. More than once he runs in horror from his own desire.

When he crosses the threshold of the bar he's been looking for, everyone turns around.

SOMETIMES

That sound belongs to a time that is gone.

Hattie McDaniel in *The Great Lie*

A girl trades her shift at the Armada theater and crosses the Pryor Mountains to hear a famous singer in a gold-leafed theater in southern Montana.

He's come from Hollywood and way out East. The voice of jealous men and prophets, kings and tyrants, laborers and former slaves. Othello and Old Joe. The Emperor Jones.

He's a star and a communist. She is my mother.

To make the house more hospitable, the heat's turned up. Everyone is sweating through the icy dusk in Sunday clothes.

She couldn't say how it began. It seemed the man took them down a long dirt path that led to a clearing, across a river, past the barbed wire of Little Tokyo, past the conquered suburban meanders and flimsy trailers of their future.

Something flooded in across the dark velvet chairs like the sun.

Here was Moses not parting the sea but walking with his people into a dark boat taken over by evil men, and now he had to lead an insurrection with his voice, and they'd come with him, following the sound across the ocean and back until it brought them to the deck where they could finally see the land where he was king, where he would repossess and set loose again all that had been captured and enslaved.

He would show them the middle ocean, a passage writ on water, in iron and alcohol, in money and blood.

When the voice slowed to a hush and it was almost over, everyone was wiping saltwater from their chins. Now they were his and he was theirs, standing in the waves.

When the man walked out of the spotlight and into the surrounding dark, the stage was emptier than anything the girl had felt. The communist had created an absence she didn't know was there.

This is what she had to say the last time I saw her alive.

When the air came to rest, folks were on their feet making all the noise they could to get this city man to walk back from the stage's dark wing into the column of light he'd filled.

When he finally crossed the floorboards of the stage, all their weeping and clapping shook the house.

Mr. Robeson would sing one last song as a gift just for the people of Billings and for the small surrounding towns, their streets emptied.

A song for the teachers and ranchers and book-read cowboys who had driven through the afternoon to feel their hearts knock against their shirts. Something for the girls who stepped carefully into their shoes.

It seemed as if what the man knew might rescue them from a trap they hadn't noticed beneath their feet. They who had thought they were already saved.

The encore was not "Old Man River" or "Amazing Grace," "Summertime" or "Abide with Me." It was a song full of unanswered questions, of witness and shared loss. A song in which an accusation lingered.

Were you there when this happened? Were you a witness to the crime?

Do you know what it sounds like when metal touches bone?

Did you watch a man become a bird, or a corpse become a man?

Were you there when they crucified my Lord? When he was taken down, or taken up, raised from concrete to abstract, earth to sky?

It's a song that witnesses a man tortured on a tree, a man who took days to die. A story on repeat.

It was sung by a man whose father had been born in bondage, who had seen his brothers in battle, who knew that a man like himself could be tied to a tree and set on fire while half the town watched.

What did the song mean to this man who organized the world with his voice?

Did the stage feel like a scaffold or a throne or some other kind of platform on the way to the end of the line?

Was it you who kissed him in the garden? You who watched from a distance as he dragged a tree up a hill?

Were you there when he reached toward the glove box?

When he tried to tell them who he was? When he lay in the street with a polished boot against his wrists?

Did you see him raise his hands?

Did you say I know this man? Did you name his name?

Did you think you saw an envelope sailing upward through the air?

Did you sweat under the lights?

Was it written on your skin?

Sometimes is the air we live in, where events and sensations are described, conditions named, ambivalence or conviction given voice.

It's where life has taken place up till now. *Sometimes* vibrates with histories intensified by subtle shifts in meaning.

You can hear it in the lines of the American spiritual repertory of the church where Paul Robeson was raised, the son of one preacher and brother of another, in the rooms where he first tried his voice.

Sometimes acknowledges a partial perspective. It is an acknowledgment of the partiality of perspective.

Sometimes may come along just to point toward a reality beyond the moment's pain. You can say to an agony: you're just passing through.

Improvisation is not the domain of any avant-garde but the underlying reality of survival.

To believe in a power that can reimagine the meanings of suffering is to cut through a wall to make a window. To build a ladder. To take off the roof.

The heart speaks to the mind, and the mind gives you a word, and the word contains a song.

The spiritual does not ask, Oh Lord, why me? It wants to know where you were and where you're going.

Sometimes is a way of thinking about a moment in relation to infinity.

It's what people say who want to find a way through.

The word stands in a doorway saying nobody knows the whole story. It started too far back.

Sometimes can be a hinge or a crossroads. The place where you can see what you've left behind and watch it all wheel away.

It dwells in a double negative. Things are not always impossible.

How many times did Mr. Robeson deliver the words of *Show Boat*, walking the constrained landscapes composed by white men who imagine what a black man might say or think or sing about *while the white folks play.*

The line, the song, the story, presents a partial view of an imaginary man. The real man who sang it on Broadway and in recording studios and opera houses didn't work on the Mississippi, but he would repeatedly be employed to play a dock worker before a live or imaginary audience.

Oscar Hammerstein II, who wrote the words to "Old Man River," graduated from Columbia Law School in 1917.

Paul Robeson, who sang his words on stage and screen, graduated from Columbia Law School in 1922.

On the concert stage Robeson would often revise Hammerstein's book, turning the abjection of the original text into statements of refusal, solidarity, and power.

The generalizing *all* of the song's racialized mind: that's miles away from *sometimes.*

Water won't always tell you where it's going. The American dividing line isn't where you think it is. Plenty of rivers pour down the east side of the Rockies, snaking north and west before they find their way to the Missouri or the Rio Grande.

The western river is more often green than brown. Not a plodding old man but a trickster who can look like anyone he chooses, there one season, not the next, sweeping away a town and drying up before the month is out.

A river speaks geographically but also temporally, revealing nearnesses and distances of mind.

Rivers write with big cursive letters. Boundaries, trade routes, passages gradually dotted with entrepôts for the people and things about to be traded or transported somewhere else.

The future is what you see when you look out over Jordan. It has its own syntax. It can talk you into a lot of things.

In Greek mythology, a river might take you to the mouth of hell.

In *The Pilgrim's Progress* a river marks the boundary between the hero's trials and his salvation. For the pilgrim's sister, it's a passage from earthly coherence into divine babble.

When the shore touches your hand, everything becomes clear. Precisely at the moment when you can no longer be understood.

Jacob met his angel on the banks of the Jordan River. Mr. Smith's angel found him by the Erie Canal. Those who followed Mr. Young named a new Jordan that emptied into an intermountain basin of salt. Jordan was the kind of river that linked the living and the dead.

Sometimes a river laps the muddy line between north and south.

Sometimes it cuts the serpentine edge between liberty and bondage.

When you cross it, you can't always go back.

Paul Robeson was born in 1898. His mother died in 1904.

Motherlessness is a condition that runs through the American blues in, above, and next to the histories of human trafficking.

The turning of children, men, women with names and histories, into futures controlled by others is driven not by a disregard for humanity but the strategic use of it.

That all languages outside the master's are deemed insurrectionist suggests how much the owning class understands the retribution it deserves. Any act against its power may be punishable by the removal of everything and everyone you love.

By the waters of Babylon, there was weeping. And in the weeping, something else.

For there they that carried us away captive required of us a song; and they that wasted us required of us mirth, saying sing us one of the songs of Zion.

In that old book, a mourning people forced into bondage have been commanded to perform a simulated happiness while the scent of all they have lost is still in the air.

What the prophets say about what's to come is the restoration of all that's been taken. Beyond the carceral demands for minstrelsy, on Jordan's other shore, all the increase, all the land, all the life that was stolen, will, when the mighty finally fall, be answered in kind, with interest.

So it is written. You can read it in the book.

The one that's endlessly rewritten and stained with blood.

Now sing. We want to hear Motherless Child.

You wouldn't have to unmake America completely to see that its Union is an act held together by its own fictions.

Huckleberry and Jim, like Robinson and Friday, live out their sentences in conflicting realities. As characters, they're looking for a future they can both survive. This is the recurrent Euro-American fantasy refuted by Euro-American histories. They live in a performance of mutuality, but what experience do they factually share?

The categorical use of one figure for cathexis and another for comic effect is among the most violent human gestures conducted by language outside the theater of war.

The sentence, in love with progress, insists on running forward.

When the motion of a plot is disturbed, temporal sequence may explode with the fragmentary truths of poetry or prophecy.

Perhaps the notion of directional movement, the plot by which histories appear to move, has become, in this moment, obsolete. What if it asks for the irrevocable destruction of conquest to be replaced by an immanent and irresistible mercy?

There is no such thing as crossing to safety. Only crossing over into new understandings of risk.

Sometimes someone asks a question of the space around them. Or the landscape asks the person.

What did the landowning Robersons of Cross Roads Township, North Carolina, have to do with William Robeson of Philadelphia and Princeton, besides giving him their name to remind him of the people who had claimed to own him.

It's been said that the Robesons and Robersons, the Robertsons and Robinsons, are branches of the same tree. Every graft leaves a scar that eventually becomes a story.

William's son Paul, who sometimes said his home was everywhere, belonged to New York and Moscow. What did he think of Billings, Montana, a place where actors and singers passed through on a road paved by all manner of art and sham? Acrobats, dancers, magicians on their way somewhere else. Con men. Circus acts. Minstrels. Prodigies. And from time to time someone altogether different. Nijinsky, Tallchief, the Barrymores. Mr. Robeson.

What did this man see when he looked out into the sweaty western concert hall? Did his voice feel the weight of everyone it carried? How does a representative belong and not belong in all the places that claim him?

He was writing a history beyond the national, beyond the constraints of imaginary borders. A history that could still produce other futures.

ENTREPÔT

On film Paul Robeson often enters through the soundtrack. Someone singing outside a window or behind a wall, a voice heard by a theater promoter in a passing car. An invisible man. A disembodied voice.

In Marseille and in London he works as a stevedore among mostly white dock workers who eat and drink at unsegregated bars and restaurants.

Where he comes from is often one of the central problems Mr. Robeson's characters confront within their stories.

In *Song of Freedom*, John Zinga is the descendant of a crazy African queen. Generations of slavery eventually land him on the London docks, wondering where he came from, wondering what his necklace means. There's a fragment of a song he can't get out of his head. He doesn't even know the words.

We see him being discovered. We see him becoming visible as white audiences embrace his art.

Now an international sensation, he tours Europe performing operatic versions of what might be his story. He's a slave or a king or a soldier, but he knows he's someone else.

We know he's someone else.

His voice punctures the composure of every scene. He's an emperor. He's an artist with a syntax of his own. He's lost until the song finds him. He will sing his way home.

The story behind the story is an Exodus in which Moses never shows up to argue on behalf of his people. He's stuck inside the Pharaoh's court.

The notebook of Negritude is filled with stories of exile and return.

I always feel the same here. Out of place. This is what Paul Robeson says to his imaginary wife, as he looks out the window of their imaginary London flat.

When he looks at the map of Africa over the fireplace, when he thinks out the window, he looks like he's almost gone.

His life is an endless sequence of themes and variations, arrivals and departures.

Within these formulaic structures, there's a flicker of home. As if running the film backward could undo its middle passages.

When John Zinga finds his way home it's through a white anthropologist who recognizes the fragment of a song that John sings as an encore.

So in the darkness of the movie palace, we are witnesses to a different kind of crime.

The singer and his wife arrive in his homeland wearing pith helmets. They hire a native valet. They want to know if anyone speaks English.

The third disc of the Criterion Collection's Paul Robeson DVD set is labeled "Pioneer."

It contains two films: *Sanders of the River* and *Jericho,* in which Robeson is a soldier whose calling is to end or fend off war.

In *Sanders of the River,* the word *pioneer* is used to describe the heroism of the British colonists, who refer to the natives as their children.

Robeson is on the other side, so to speak, of the River. A Liberian thief who eventually shows his greatness in the service of the crown.

The encounter between white direction and black embodiment intensifies the furious smile of the film's "natural man." The costume that touches the actor's skin includes a tail. The pioneer will refuse to sit through its gala premier.

Later he will say, "Speak of me as I am."

He'll say, "Let me fly."

For two days in 1938 Robeson's voice took down a wall: while both sides listened, it stopped the Spanish Civil War.

In the 1940s, he sang the national anthem with Oakland shipbuilders; met with the commissioner of baseball to argue on behalf of black players, including Jackie Robinson; met with President Truman about the need for an anti-lynching law; and broadcast *Ballad for Americans.* He announced his departure from the film industry in protest of its racism.

In the 1950s, he was blacklisted, erased from the public records of his alma mater, targeted by the FBI, and CIA, and MI5, and prohibited from international travel.

Not a man without a country but a man whose country had set out to to make him disappear.

Around the time Paul Robeson announced his departure from the stage, Jackie Robinson played his first major league game for the Brooklyn Dodgers.

The fact that Robinson was later named Rookie of the Year only widened the division between his enemies and his fans.

I'm thinking of a political cartoon from 1949. Jackie Robinson is looking toward the horizon, at Paul Robeson's enormous footprints, which are walking off the map.

Is Robinson a 20th-century Crusoe, newly shipwrecked in Brooklyn, anxious to encounter signs of a native presence with whom he must reckon? Or is he sheepishly following a path the larger-than-life Robeson worked so hard to establish?

Is he hesitant because Robeson is an object lesson, brutally beaten by his football teammates at Rutgers, though he survived to play professionally to support himself in law school?

Does Robinson view Robeson's presence as a threat, albeit one that might possess crucial information for his survival? Are these the footprints of a fugitive who can't be bothered to cover his own tracks or of a genius who's so far ahead of the game that he's too small to see?

In the cartoon, Jackie Robinson, whose testimony before HUAC was damning of Robeson, is carrying a cartoon gun.

Pearl S. Buck: In our country . . .

Eslanda Goode Robeson: Which country?

Eslanda Goode Robeson: Your America and mine are not the same.

Pearl S. Buck: Maybe there isn't any America at all.

FRIEND & FELLOW WORKER

to remember their bigotry accurately
to cease to dream about lions which always is
to dream about them, I put my hand in the lion's mouth
to assuage its anger....

Bernadette Mayer

If one says "Red"
and there are 50 people listening,
it can be expected that there will be 50 reds in their minds.
And one can be sure that all these reds will be very different.

Josef Albers, *Interaction of Colors*

In March 1947 at a concert in Salt Lake City, Paul Robeson sang "The Ballad of Joe Hill," an elegy and rallying cry for the labor organizer and poet who was framed for murder and executed in the same city before he had a chance to fight the bosses of the local mines.

It's a song about a man who was mourned but never died, who didn't stop until he turned into an anthem.

That night Robeson announced he would soon be leaving the stage. Not just this one but all of them.

When the song's final note had rippled through the concert hall, there was a half-minute in which you could hear nothing but a room so wide it could almost hide a crime.

By design, the center point of Salt Lake City is the corner of
Temple and State streets, where the blinding light reflected
off the salt flats knocks against the granite of a square block of
religious and corporate architecture.

When the Mormons established the State of Deseret on the
portion of the Ute homeland then claimed by Mexico, they gave it
its own phonetic alphabet and golden coins imprinted with lions
and a beehive to remind its emigrants to get busy when they got
there. Deseret soon became Utah Territory, though Utah Territory
eventually upcycled its theocracy for statehood so the US military
would set down its guns or point them in other directions.

The powers residing at the territorial headquarters would convert
their history of peculiarity into zealous assimilation, making
themselves as white and profitable as possible.

But other things on which church and state could not agree
were occurring at the same time. One was the development of an
extraction industry that brought in non-Mormon prospectors and
corporate interests.

The other was the development of a socialist party, which pleased
neither church nor state nor speculators nor bosses.

Those who had already developed their own forms of resource
exploitation and social order, had mixed feelings about seeing
them managed outside their jurisdiction.

In pursuit of a unified image of goodness: a flash of homogenous,
stage-lit abundance.

A shining, shiny coin at the bottom of a mountain pass.

*

Mining had begun in Utah at least as far back as 1847, first stone, then lead and iron.

Then silver and copper. By 1906 money from the East was paying miners to dig the Bingham mine that would eventually become the biggest scar on earth.

The mine owners and sugar makers continued to feed their state-sanctioned power in what was now a state that had traded its most self-evident peculiarities for a chance at looking normal.

*

Among the losses in the assimilation process were the socialist practices begun by early Mormons in Ohio and Illinois and Missouri and carried out to small Utah towns, whereby property would be deeded to the church and individuals would receive in return what they needed, whether that was more or less than they had given.

They didn't want to depend on strangers or governments whose stance toward them could turn on the politics of a moment; they wanted to live in a circle of shared sufficiency.

A version of the practice survived in the form of a welfare system supplied by church-run farms and distributed by local congregations.

In the 1860s and 1870s, towns like Brigham City, where Eliza Snow's niece Virginia lived with her mother, were almost fully self-sufficient.

Virginia eventually left the church but carried its socialist dream into political action.

The Mormon Church was initially against mining ventures, which some believed might overwhelm the state's electorate with non-Mormon voters.

Eventually mining won, over both Mormon and international socialism.

By the time Joe Hill arrived in the Salt Lake Valley, the land of the Utes had been developed into the largest network of extraction sites in the world.

FRIEND & FELLOW WORKER

Joel Emmanuel Hägglund sailed from Sweden to New York at twenty-two, just after the century had turned. He worked his way East to West and hung on in San Francisco when the earth shook it hard in 1906.

He was Joseph Hillström for a while before he joined the International Workers of the World and became Joe Hill.

He knew a bit of music and took up songwriting on the road.

In 1911, he wrote "The Preacher and the Slave," a critique of proselytizing religions that exploited everyday folk as much as the bosses of industry, offering nothing but "pie in the sky."

He wrote songs about waking up, digging in, standing up, moving on.

He wrote organizing lyrics to be sung to recognizable melodies, so anyone could ride along. They were dance hall songs and drinking songs and hymns.

There was "Casey Jones." "It's a Long Way Down to the Soupline." "Ta-Ra-Ra Boom De-Ay." And the Salt Lake City favorite, "Nearer My Job to Thee."

Behind the song was a question that you could answer in the singing: what was your relation to the boss? To the man upstairs? The man with the view who saw men crawl out of the earth in the distance, looking like the dirt they rose from, as natural as hell.

In 1913, Mr. Hill arrived in Utah to work and organize at the Silver King Mine in Park City.

He found a home and a girlfriend among the Swedish community in Murray, Utah, a town whose politics were for a time also dominated by socialists.

One night a man was killed, and Joe Hill was picked up on shaky evidence.

He refused to defend himself on the grounds that it might hurt the reputation of a young woman. After all, in the absence of proof, all men were innocent.

Friend and F. W. is the way Joe Hill addressed most of the letters he sent from the Salt Lake City jail.

He wrote to Elizabeth Gurley Flynn, whom he called Rebel Girl.

He wrote to Big Bill Haywood and to Katie Phar, who sang for the Union in Spokane.

In his own defense, all he said was that he had lived like an artist and would die like one.

He said he'd rather play the fiddle than eat.

He said it's up to you.

He wrote to his Friend and Fellow Worker, Sam Murray: *I don't know anything new and hoping you are successful snaring the elusive doughnut, I remain, Yours for the O. B. U.*

One. Big. Union.

Mr. Hill didn't want to be a man with any kind of badge. He didn't want to be held up or pinned down. He wanted to walk down the street and whistle at the desert night.

Virginia Snow Stephen—the daughter of a prophet—was an artist and labor sympathizer.

After Joe Hill was sentenced, she was able to convince a Denver attorney to handle his appeal, which failed anyway.

He was shot by firing squad at the Penitentiary and work farm in the section of Salt Lake City known as Sugar House, near where Mr. Roberts lived and where he too had been briefly imprisoned.

Virginia Snow was born in 1864 to Mary Elizabeth Houtz, the seventh wife of Lorenzo Snow, the brother of Eliza Snow who had not yet become a prophet of the church to which they all belonged.

As a young woman, the younger Miss Snow studied art, then taught it. At some point, she left the church and joined the socialist cause.

At the advanced age of twenty-eight, Miss Snow married a Mr. Stephen, but they divorced five years later. She taught at the University of Utah for two decades.

Arguing against capital punishment, Mrs. Stephen wrote: *If it is evil to kill in the heat of passion, is it not a double evil to kill by a supine community consent called law?*

When the law was embodied by community acquiescence or consent, to what higher laws might one appeal?

When police shot and killed another unarmed Wobbly, Roy J. Horton, a month before Joe Hill was executed, she sang at his funeral too.

A few months later, she was relieved of her position on the university's art faculty, moved further West, and disappeared almost entirely from the public record.

How do you like her art?

Everyone needs some kind of healing.

Here in Babylon, there's sugar on the wound.

It's going to burn a little.

It's going to hurt some more before it feels better.

CLOSE ENCOUNTERS

Among the mouth-breathing children and instant potatoes, the patience of Teri Garr slides from irritation into pity behind the local milk carton.

The man across from her looks up from the Wyoming landscape he has made with his fork on the flat earth before him.

I guess you've noticed something ... a little strange with Dad, is what the man says to the ring of subjects with whom he shares this tiny country. *It's okay though. I'm still Dad.*

When these words travel across the confused void of the kitchen, he has the felt sense of a calling without understanding what it is. The king is mad but he's still in charge.

I can't describe it, says a mouth that has almost lost its words. *But what I'm feeling....*

We watch him sweat through what looks like his last dinner with the disciples.

The table is a map to something.

Everyone searches for the line between delusion and prophecy. Where's dad among the gamma rays and psychopathologies of the nuclear family.

Who will jump ship and who will be onboard when the next storm electrifies the air around them.

This is the place, he thinks, staring at the pale tectonic plate rising up to meet him.

Reverse the angle. It's Teri Garr having visions and playing the fool with her food. She's sweating like a sailor but she's still Mom.

The Equal Rights Amendment introduced in 1921 and nearly ratified in 1971 is undergoing further debate on the floor of a house in Indiana.

Who among the executive orders hears her cry. Who backs away from the table to make a call. Who buys her a jacket with unnaturally long arms.

In a structural analysis of religious experience, those who are chosen move to the other end of the sentence; subjects become objects dwarfed by the invisible vectors that drive them. Real is what rearrange they. Them rearrange out inside.

When Roy Neary sees the igneous intrusion above the Belle Fourche River on television, he knows every word in the newscaster's mouth is a lie.

Our man's getting warmer. The landscape he had no words for, the one buried in his food, is exploding onto a 1:1 map of the world.

Two kinds of knowing approach the same horizon.

That he lost his job at the power company is a fact slowly crossing from description into metaphor. The stroke of night air offers him a new category. In the game logic of a government agency, he is now It.

When someone asks It what he wants, all he wants is to know It is real. We're standing with him at the edge of gaslight in the full electronic regalia of revelation.

They're called pilgrims, and he's one of them. They wear flags and sunglasses and move robotically through the parted multitudes.

He's greeted by girls from Mobile who've spent hours in makeup becoming creatures that can lead him to his own future as a child. Their rubbery suits cause them to giggle as they totter toward him, as they take his hand.

Military protocol tries to make it a hostage exchange but all the rubber-suited girls want is him. That everyone sees this—that there are witnesses—is a vindication eclipsed only by the radiance of the man's joy.

The mouth of the mothership becomes a real mouth edged with well-lit teeth.

Dad recognizes a new syntax older than memory.

He steps onto her tongue like a three-letter word.

The site of a geological extrusion on sacred land in the middle of the American island is reconstructed in Alabama as the location for a film about translation.

Who will encounter whom in Matȟó Thípila or in the cinematic dark of its replica?

Is the film a re-enactment of first contact or a template for the future performed in the vibrating present?

Who is a native of Indiana and who is lost in translation?

The alien French who named the Belle Fourche River have sent a filmmaker into the future to play a linguist translating between the latest crowd of pickup-drivers and a new wave of aliens whose intentions are as unclear as ever.

No representatives of Matȟó Thípila appear or are mentioned on screen. No one at the re-enactment knows their language.

The name of the lead alien, played by the daughter of the film's key grip, does not appear in the credits. Her most famous role, years later, is that of a dead body.

EARTHWORK

LABYRINTH

A pattern seen from above has one kind of clarity.

From above there is a way out of the labyrinth.

On the ground you begin with a spider's thread.

On the ground you let go, or hold on, to follow a crooked line you can hardly see.

I don't have a bird's-eye view. I don't see the earthly flower from the sky.

In the middle of the Crimean War, not the first and not the last, a nurse uplifted and weighed down by undergarments noticed more bodies dying in hospitals than in the fields.

In order to get the attention of the men who both oversaw and overlooked her work, she pulled her data into the kind of diagrammatic flower called a rose chart, though it appears less like a rose than a strip mine.

The war was, like most wars, a religious war played out by national coalitions that at some point seemed to forget why they were there.

Nationalism will mobilize around religious ideals even when those ideals are surrogates for less easily justified motives such as ownership of what is known or believed to be underground.

The battle for a particular view is sometimes driven by those who would rather destroy it than share what they see.

*

At the turn of the 20th century, W. E. B. Du Bois presented to the Paris Exhibition his research on black life in America as living information.

His data works were, like Ms. Nightingale's, both portraiture and landscape, a vision of material reality that gave material voice to the failures of reconstruction.

The work of the data portraits is the work of perspective. A crosscut interval, a working of art.

To make of what is already known a revelation, a formal pressure toward the work of consciousness.

Rearrange what you know to make a new version of the visionary, the prophetic, the inspired, the revelatory. To see the tired facts anew.

To what end?

So as not to repeat history in oblivion, writes Theresa Cha.

Look at the Bingham mine off Utah's I-15, and you'll see a hole whose downward spiral is visible from space. A wound big enough to surpass the past's ability to correct itself.

When the desert was told to blossom like a rose, this is the dark flower it became.

Its form rhymes with the mythic labyrinth later echoed in Robert Smithson's *Spiral Jetty*.

On your way to the jetty, you'll pass the Golden Spike monument, purported to unify one of the continent's nations by rail.

At the edge of the salty lake, who or what is being joined or pulled apart, extracted or buried.

A landscape of extractable wealth and all its underworlds. The earth as a body; its bodies treated like dirt.

Watch Paul Robeson playing a miner, and you will see the touch of economics on a living surface.

Histories rewired, unrepaired.

From above, the jetty looks like a fiddlehead fern. A mineral fern at the lip of an unfreezeable inland sea.

Or a tightly wound question on the tip of a tongue.

*

Mr. Smithson's spiral jetty places a mirror before Dante's textual spirals.

A divine comedy is a systematic view of spiritual progress, of crimes and punishments.

It is a comedy because nobody dies within its diagrammatic terraces. They live forever in the messes they've made.

Smithson was fascinated by mirrors. In their simulated infinity, they reveal some truths and hide others.

Sometimes the medium is not the only message. He was interested in what could and couldn't be reversed.

The spiral jetty is on the other side of Jordan from the Bingham mine.

Like the artist's non-sites in the nearby Bonneville salt flats, the jetty is a replication and inversion of Mr. Young's mythic claim at the entrance to Emigration canyon: *This is the place.*

It's within the Earthly Tragedies of US mythology that Mr. Smithson has been placed by history. But oppositional categories are not the only way of seeing.

His dialectical thinking holds a place for unknowing and ungoverned possibility beyond the clash of opposites still generated by US expressionism and expansionism.

This is the place. And it is not.

How far will the hinge of conjunction open.

Archives are the embodied essence of the event, wrote Robert Smithson.

But archives aren't boundless; they cannot contain the fullness of a time or place. Like art, they are defined by limits as well as by unseen depths.

They are selections as well as depositories and dumping grounds; they are built.

They may be framed by an argument. They value some things over others, full of contradictions in their acts of salvage, disposal, and dispersal, their raising up or casting out of realia.

Anyone decides over and over what to keep and what to throw away, as you decide over and over who you are and what you do.

As a figure in a landscape, you define a relation to the world; you define the word *world* around it.

An archive, like a temple, is a species of theater where roles and patterns are refolded and remade in a likeness of history.

If you drive from the jetty or the mine through the city toward Little Cottonwood Canyon, you'll approach without reaching the Granite Mountain Records Vault which holds the genealogical and other records of the church from which the city radiates.

When energy is devoted to remembering one thing, it is also in the business of forgetting something else.

From where will renewal come to us—to us who have defiled and emptied the whole earthly globe? asks Simone Weil. *From the past alone, if we love it.*

I had to stop writing in order to clean my desk.

I had to stop writing to speak with the angel of dust.

The card I pull is strength not speed.

Something in the body reaching for something outside it.

I'm looking for the wave that rises like a wall. Reaching for Octavia Butler's prophecies, not science, not fiction but the capacity for thought beyond narrative event and recorded fact.

A field that can think about what a feeling knows.

Parables are tools of directed attention. One part moves around outside you, the other circumnavigates your blood. A story reading you as you read it.

Where does it—the It that is also you—come to rest?

What risks do you feel at the threshold, where do you place the fear that you won't come back from wherever it's taking you, the It that is thought.

I'm watching a serrated line move across the map. The sound of a finger pointing away from what it's done.

I'm listening for the bell, for the machine to stop, dishes in the kitchen, the sound of a person I love, my system crashing as the sprung door bangs shut.

In the imperfect wobble of the glass that separates my desk from the world outside, a woman stops on the sidewalk across the street.

She wears two large backpacks—one facing forward, the other back—and carries a large shopping bag in each hand. When she pauses, she sets down the two bags in her hands but leaves her packs on.

How often have I had a private moment in public space, aware of how easily I could wander out of one category and into another.

It was Linnaeus who broke the world into three varieties he called kingdoms, but he owed most of the breaking to Aristotle.

Who is the king of the kingdom, who says what distinguishes the crow from the grass or from the petrochemical waste in which my food is wrapped?

It occurs to me that any situation may demand the reinvention of both self and relation, what it means and what it costs to hold something together.

One path or another blows up before or behind my limited view of the road.

The condition of empathy in Octavia Butler's speculation is a disability in the world at large and a superpower for the writer as long as she can survive the impact of the violence that surrounds her.

Her list of persecuted outsiders in US reactionary history includes the Mormons.

It is clear in her novel-parables that it is Butler, not her protagonist, who is writing the scripture in which her text is grounded. Or rather, one writer exists within another.

Earthseed is the essential practice of making something from or on a different ground.

Here is a path, here is where I fell, don't let feeling throw you off your game.

Yes, it is too much. Turn the page over. Write it down.

I have lived on both sides of the continental divide but most of my adult tears have flowed into the Atlantic.

I want to know death and yet live to tell it. I want to know the border.

I want to stick my foot out of the bed. To feel the presence of the world with detached compassion.

I want to emerge from the heat of the car forever.

I want to lie down between the cool lines and sleep in the pages of a book.

Charles Reznikoff, of Manhattan and Los Angeles, said: "I didn't invent the world, but I felt it."

When another person says out loud the words you have inside you, a sticky, silky bond forms between you.

I am a leaf on your tree as you are on mine.

You whom I don't know, I feel you in my skin. You've been holding my hand while I slept. I've been leaning against you all along. It was your nearness that made the train's clatter sound like a lullaby.

Wherever we are will be a house forever. I feel your breath against my neck. O fearless comrade, our bed is made of awe.

ANYTHING GOES

As if all the Heavens were a Bell, and Being but an Ear

Emily Dickinson

Here's a map before it comes into focus. Just before it decides how to say where you are.

Blue veins, red arteries, a nerve net. A spine. A shoulder. A heart.

If you're driving to the airport from the northern hills, skirting the lake, turning sharply to the west, it's hard not to follow the reflective white arrow of the left exit toward Reno.

A wheel wants to turn like an arch wants a brick. Gradually the mind sets down the weight of everything else.

The curve pulling like an idea surrendering to a narrative arc. Someone's name on a page too large to see. Was this so long ago called destiny?

"I" for interstate means an Eisenhower belief system. A general, a president wanting to supply the future with this relentless thump.

Dominion and dividing lines remade as Access. Space obliterated for the sake of Time.

This is what it offers, what does it extract.

Look at the anchor of this line against the valley. A mountain face on one side—a taut, open plain on the other.

The mark where Kennecott Copper took the foothills. The land stripped down to elements. A romance written just beneath the map's pale yellow and pixilated green.

Here's what the story said in the middle of the road that cuts the middle of the map: This is not mine. I am not its heroine, not its witness, not its heir but somehow part of its dirt, its salt, its sulfurous air.

In the eye of a true missionary lies a picture of collective generosity. If you took the time to see it their way, you would understand, you would come over. Let the current take you.

Only such peculiar magic could push the valley into flower out of the darkness of a hat. Even the mirage is brine. Camouflage disintegrating into blinding white.

If you look up, you can see you are at the bottom of a pyramid.

From here its hushed opulence might look like divine compensation for good earthly works.

Look at this family by its un-lit brick fireplace. Exemplary, entrepreneurial. Showing, not telling.

It's there in the car rental employee's ebullience, her desperate efficiency. As if I have passed through a veil to reach her, and she's been waiting for me on the other side of her counter. Well-dressed, able to give clear directions. Aware of being watched.

If she has to explain the terms of the insurance, her performance has been a failure. She wants me to accept the protection she is offering or weather will threaten to fall from her skies.

In the middle of the book, my parents disappeared.

They didn't fall sleep inside a lucite capsule or walk onto the tongue of a large metal mouth; they landed on a concrete shore definitive as Plymouth.

Bits of them joined the molecular remains of dinosaurs and ferns that powered the indebted heap they drove because someone had convinced them it was practically free. Bits of them in the yes and no of a nine-minute file.

An image becomes part of you when its projection hits your skin or you feel its writing on a white-washed wall.

She's being pulled on a sled down an icy road behind a puffy sedan. The trout he's caught is gasping for water. The world is full of proof.

He's holding a broom that's taller than he is. He's riding with his brothers in a cart pulled by a goat while the ceiling lifts away, not as I imagined.

She's nervous on horseback in a tightly buckled blouse. This is the place, and it is not. Site and non-site, in the midsummer sun of the road they were born on.

In the middle of a book is a gutter. The place where all the pages disappear.

The edges are margins. The borders, where we live.

A rock may withstand anything but water, anything but wind. Even when you're anchored to a place, the world will surge and crash around you.

Their car came to rest a half-hour away from the cave where Mr. Sessions outlived the snow of 1848. Somewhere north of the Spiral Jetty and its nearby superfund sites, postscripts to the history of mining.

I save the file over and over as if something has changed. It is where my breath pauses.

When I look at Robert Smithson's unfinished ramp outside of Amarillo, Texas, I think it is the perfect embodiment of rising and falling.

A fragment of another jetty. A modern translation of the ancient labyrinth that for a moment made of an imprisoned man a bird.

I was on my way to meet them with embarrassed reluctance. I was bringing them a book called *Alive*.

The jetty said: Go back, not forward. Turn in the opposite direction of everything that brought you here. Get dizzy till you fall.

As my mother in heaven reached up to fix her hair, I watched my sister's mouth form words I couldn't understand.

The sound of my mother became a bell looking for the wind.

In her blood was Benadryl and a caffeine supplement.

On her feet the smudged coral lacquer of an amateur pedicure.

Against her skin, the pearl-like buckshot from a shattered bag of water softener they'd found on sale.

On her tongue I don't know. Her mouth of shattered glass, wired shut by the body artist assigned to disguise the realities of death.

Beloved is the liquidated building surrounded by the windblown grass.

Blessed are the zeroes of the clock passing through the one.

If a life were a book, what kind of book would it be?

This one's in pencil with a drifting hand.

On a phone I keep in the closet: five messages. A treatise behind a series of repetitions.

The feeling, repeatedly, that she was on the verge of disclosing something. A sudden softness in her tone.

The act of forgetting may transform one wound into another. A gash within the physical world, now translated to a lapse in memory.

What heals is not made whole, what's missing is not replaced but added to. It is more not less than it once was.

Healing is hidden. The opposite of revelation.

On the Metro-North train between White Plains and Harlem,
I'm lost in bubbling pictograms half-hidden by city councils in
battleship and gunmetal.

Linda from Craigslist calls me a believer but doesn't say of what.

I observe this like a passing train from a passing building.

What all I want to forgive is what the world is.

A train called Tear of the Clouds goes by fast then falls behind.
It shakes me up while someone looks down from a chain-linked
overpass, a pause in the prerecorded story of the day.

Behind the Tear of Clouds is Sojourner Truth. Sojourner Truth
is stopped at Harlem. She's the second car with the sun on her
starboard paneling. She's aluminum and fine. She's steel with a
wide blue stripe.

In a sudden blast of sun, a man is reading *Living with a SEAL* as I
read his watch.

These words are a deflection, like the clock, from a howling
interior.

Where is the sojourner who gave this to me, who stood for half a
minute in the place my mother was?

SOMETIMES

A few years after her trip to Paul Robeson's concert in Billings, my mother entered the University of Mr. Young.

I see her at a distance, in miniature: dynamite surrounded by dry grass.

She's squinting toward the sun in a homemade suit with shoulder pads and fancy buttons and a kick-pleated pencil skirt hemmed just below the knee. She is only half-hiding her beautiful legs.

She's coming into focus inside a crystal ball, tiny and magnified. She looks like Dorothy in Oz—a little frightened, a little in the clouds, unsure if this is her destiny or she's just passing through.

Where am I standing when I see this? A mother might ask a fortune teller for news of a lost child, but it's not where a child would go to find a mother who is trying to usher her into a future all the more vast for being undone.

The picture is edgeless and familiar. Its order, its strange costumes, its secrets, are like those of other imaginary cities, a version of the place the tornado left behind.

When my mother returned to her parents' house, most of her friends had married and moved to the towns where their husbands were raised.

I see at this crossroads that she might have headed East or further West. I can imagine her choosing to argue with the gods. But as far as I know, she did not.

Instead, the horse she had ridden down Main Street took her further into a story in which she did more or less what was expected of her. She had only stopped to pick some flowers. She would press them into a book and put the book back on a shelf.

When I watch my mother in this way, I see what I felt when I arrived at Mr. Young's University in a homemade skirt hemmed just below the knee.

Sometimes I was two people, one watching the other, a more seasoned actor helping an understudy with her lines.

I am thinking about the blur between oneself and one's category, the individual present conflated with a collective past, the imaginary futures for which a real body might at times feel responsible. Might at times be responsible.

It was my father who taught me that land could be read like an archive.

Whatever I know about the Belle Fourche River I owe to him.

He taught me to fish. And taught, as I have, other people, comma, the children of.

As a boy, he watered the elephants for a ticket to the circus.

His mother hired him out with his brothers to perform musical numbers for funerals and garden clubs.

At some point, he tap danced in a lounge, breathing in the shadows on one side of the curtain and feeling the raw pleasure of stepping out into the light.

He enlisted as a teenager and slowly lost his hearing from the shelling of world war. In him I thought I saw an ongoing desire to walk away.

When my father played piano, there was always one song. It wasn't until I was older that I knew what it was.

He couldn't remember how he learned it or where he'd heard it first.

He never sang the words until he started to lose them, stopping halfway through, afraid of where his forgetting might take him. *You ain't been blue.*

Until you've felt that ... No, no, no.

Indigo's first use in English was in 1289. Its effect as a dye is unstable, its depth a record of duration. It moves from plant to paper, to skin, to cotton. It's in the grain of William Morris rugs and silk kimonos and the thread of midnight cotton-club tuxedos.

Sometimes a word will saturate everything it touches.

When my father was seven, he was left tied to a tree upside down. He remembered it to the last. Right down to his shoes.

When overcome by an encounter with something beyond words, he openly wept.

He sure was a cute little bugger, said my uncle, last summer.

I wish we had talked about Broca's Paradox.

There is a kind of blue that, in order to see it, you have to look away.

I can accept the notion that I have lost myself only if I imagine that someone is holding my hand. . . . Holding someone's hand has always been my idea of joy.

The Passion According to Clarice Lispector

I don't like endings. I hate to say goodbye. The trouble's in my blood.

When I spoke on the phone with my mother, the signal that she had something else to do was a reiterated sequence involving the word *love*. Loose threads of talk were stitched into place while we batted the word back and forth until one of us hung up.

After her father died, when her mother was living in an apartment in Salt Lake City, one of our family visits ended in the parking lot with my grandmother in a shimmering raven-colored dress, dabbing her face with a handkerchief, then gripping my mother's arm through the car window, demanding to know how we could leave her like this. I was in the back of the overloaded station wagon facing her as we pulled away. It was my job to wave until she was too small to see.

In Carl Dreyer's film *Ordet*, the mad prophet Johannes wanders in and out of scenes devoted to the stories of others. When he says, *I build these houses but no one lives in them*, the line is as devastating as a death in the family. Can anyone live in an invisible house? In a poem? In a book? Can you live there and still have your own story?

Narrative resists such a person. Johannes is always departing. His family thinks reading Kierkegaard drove him mad. They blow out the candles he lights; they don't say goodbye. He's living in a book they don't read.

There is no fixed liturgy in the church I came up in. During a service, the only word said in unison is *Amen*. It passes as quickly as a schoolbell. Everyone is altogether thinking about lunch. I want an Amen that means *I read you* or *You've got it*, and *I back you all the way*.

The ending of every story is artificial, a matter of framing. After all, we've survived it. It continues without us. Even in an epic, we witness just a glimpse of the total picture. So much is gestured toward or implied, out of sight.

In a poem, closure is a matter of sound. The larger work's horizon is immeasurably distant, concurrent with, or parallel to one's very life and breath. The goodbye is implied. Its conjugated love is a contract with the reader. *Here, I made this for you.* I'm with you in this meadow, in this house.

You find a clearing in the thicket. You build the structure you can build, or you sweep clean the spaces someone else has left behind. You stake all your hope that someone will arrive and warm this paper house with their presence.

I love you. I mean that. I know you have to go.

This book has many origins and many unwritten ends.

One early thread emerged from a 1926 essay in which Robert Walser compares a liontamer to a Mormon polygamist whose wives only appear to obey for the sake of public performance. Walser's essay led me deeper into an ongoing archival entanglement with Mormonism, which led into further questions about civic governance and categorical exclusion; historical elisions around women's experience; intersections of race, class, and sexuality; extraction economies; and concurrent performances of family in theater, early film, and everyday life. Worlds within the world.

Walser wrote two other pieces on the subject, one devoted to the lion as an actor, the other on liontaming as a legacy of expertise mysteriously transmitted from father to son. Walser wanted to be an actor. He was fascinated by clothing—the transformative power of costumes, the erotics of fabric touching the skin—and its role in the staging of selfhood. His attention to performance met my interest in the role of theater and film in breaking or buttressing social norms, including who and how we love, what we worship, and with whom we belong.

Other threads of modernist imagination run through the substrata of the book. One is Gertrude Stein's *Four in America*, which rewrites the biographies of four major American figures with reassigned identities: a remaking of national narratives composed twenty years after her *Making of Americans*. Another is William Carlos Williams's assertion that "Poetry is a rival government, always in opposition to its cruder replicas." The line appears in an essay Williams wrote in 1940 imagining a conversation with his brother, the architect Edgar Irving Williams. In its assertion of poetry's alliance—or potential alliance—with other forms of political action I heard references not only to the Resistance to fascism in Europe but also resistance to the colonial status of Puerto Rico, their mother's homeland.

Some of this work emerged from my ongoing interest in blacklists, poetic dictation, and other intersections of prophecy and heresy. I wanted to understand the criteria by which a member is cast out of an organization that claims to be rooted in tolerance and inclusiveness. How could one account for the speed with which Paul Robeson went from being the exemplary American voice (especially in the widely broadcast *Ballad for Americans*) to being an exemplary un-American?

The blacklists of the 1950s showed me one part of Paul and Eslanda Robeson's world; their film work with the modernist poet H.D. and her circle another. My mother's memory of hearing Robeson when she was a teenager led back into Robeson's touring repertoire, including the ballad celebrating Joe Hill, who sought to unionize the Utah mines. Hill was born the same year as my great-grandmother. They both died in Salt Lake City: she in 1983 in her 104th year and he in 1915, executed for a murder he didn't commit.

I came into the world through a religion based on testimony and witnessing. The loosely stitched lines between seen and unseen worlds have been with me as long as I can remember. But testimony, whether residing in churches or courtrooms, is based in sensory knowledge, and the underpinnings of that knowledge are seldom clear. Similarly, the witnessing that takes place in cinema and theater is intertwined with the neurological and ideological networks of desire and belief. What feels true—and what makes it so?

Some of this book's other threads come from family records, including the missionary journal and photographic archive of Hyrum Bischoff, my great-uncle, whose collaboration with B. H. Roberts in 1924 resulted in what seems to be the Mormon church's first missionary film, now lost.

One of my mother's great-grandmothers emigrated to the Salt Lake Valley after a childhood working in the Scottish mines, and in her seventies performed the highland fling—a dance developed not as a rite of courtship but as a prelude to war—at a resort near the eventual site of Robert Smithson's *Spiral Jetty*. Her daughter was a bit player who worked briefly with Maude Adams in the Salt Lake City Theatre.

A generation earlier, a midwife named Patty Bartlett Sessions had said she recognized Joseph Smith from a dream. Magnetized by his new religion, she and her husband joined the migration to Ohio, Illinois, Missouri, and eventually Utah. Their son Perrigrine served as a bodyguard for Joseph Smith, to whom both his mother and sister were privately married. It was Perrigrine Sessions's polygamous household in which my great-grandmother Patty Sessions Hatch (1879–1983) was raised.

Other narratives unfolded when I moved to Iowa City, the mid-nineteenth century terminus of the railroad, where poorer emigrants outfitted handcarts they then pulled to Utah. Ezekiel Clark, who assisted and profited from the Mormon emigration, married Patty Sessions's daughter Sylvia. After the Civil War, Clark was purportedly responsible for convincing Salmon P. Chase to adopt "greenback" dollars, unsupported by gold or silver and printed in green ink as if they might grow on trees. As if money were as natural and holy as a leaf.

In the church's early decades, populist commentary linked Mormons with racial otherness and miscegenation, as documented in the work of W. Paul Reeve. In 1838 at the time of the Indian Removal Act and the Mormon Extermination Order, the possibilities of a Mormon alignment with native peoples made them a political as well as a social threat, but critiques of the religion focused on sex.

Polygamy continued to dominate the public perception of Mormonism in ways that occluded both the significance of women's speech and writing and the concurrent practice of polyandry. Many of Joseph Smith's wives (including Patty and Sylvia Sessions) were simultaneously married to other men, and the practice of proxy marriages, sealings, and adoptions further complicated the practice of family.

Mormon earnestness and optimism and the concept of an extra-planetary afterlife have generated an impressive number of comic, tragi-comic, tragic, and enraged essays, YouTube channels, comedy routines, and plays. The underlying theme of which is often: How could anyone believe this?

I wanted to understand what drew women like Patty Sessions and Eliza Snow—and Sojourner Truth, who joined the self-declared Prophet Matthias in a smaller sect around the same time—into what appeared from a distance more like thralldom than an assertion of radical feminist identity. At closer range, the proposal of an interracial, multi-partnered communal site of devotion based in ongoing revelation suggested more interesting options than the church and state that criminalized sexual freedom outside of the bounds of nuclear marriage. Did they see the conceptual failure of the American Union and choose to collaborate with others in its rewriting? How deeply did these new structures betray them? What were the alternatives?

The first decade of the twenty-first century saw an alignment of advocates for same-sex marriage and fundamentalist polygamous communities, both seeking to undo the definition of marriage dictated by the Defense of Marriage Act signed into law during the Clinton administration. The Mormon church—still working to shake off its association with non-normative unions—joined with other religious interests in a well-funded campaign for California's Proposition 8, which would have overturned the state's legalization of same-sex marriage.

What other alliances, I wondered, might be possible in a non-binary sociopolitical world?

My interest in the line between poetry written by women and prophecy delivered by men led me to Eliza Snow then to Snow's brother Lorenzo, with whom she traveled to Egypt and Palestine, and his daughter Virginia, the socialist, artist, and activist who tried to save Joe Hill from execution.

Poetry is drawn to destabilizing established patterns of thought, to making visible the power to see otherwise. It seeks to bend the recursive loops of history toward futures other than those that this nation's governing bodies repeatedly instruct its citizens to accept.

This undoing and remaking is an ancient task. It's in the recorded tales of Penelope's unweaving, in Circe's gravitational pull away from heroism and war and her transformation of warriors into lovers. It's in Arachne's nonlinear webbing and Ariadne's brilliant circumventing of the labyrinth's mysteries with a single thread. It's in Eduardo Galeano's reassembling of other contradictory American histories in his *Memory of Fire* trilogy. It's in the instructive histories of midwifery and medicine and other practices indebted to indigenous knowledge. It's in the deep historical and cultural work of W. E. B. Du Bois. It's in the writing on the wall.

How can speculative thinking turn inevitabilities into new patterns of redistributed power?

I ask this of a future that will outlive me. I feel it in the smoke darkening the air of horses too close to the interstate's whine and in the large-fanned, lit-up warehouses of creatures in confinement, lives also inseparable from ours.

This work is also informed by what I touched, breathed, saw, and heard in my childhood. I didn't live in the Rocky Mountain West where Mormonism had been mainstreamed, but my family ties often returned me to that geography. I wanted to see behind the facades of its disciplinary, cautionary, simulated past. My siblings and I were raised as a peculiar family who belonged, at a distance, to this "peculiar people." We were to be alternately exemplary and invisible, available for service and intimately unreachable. This book is also the result of the contemplation and questioning that developed in the silence I often felt compelled to keep.

As a child, I was haunted by the notion of "outer darkness": the afterlife designated for those who have access to the Truth but turn away from it.

The spirit world is a social environment from which individual detachment is perilous and irrevocable.

The Mormon afterlife, like the story of *Lost in Space*, is founded in a view of social reinvention, but both are caught in colonial justifications of ascendancy and dominance. Those who, through their behavior on Earth, achieve a godlike perfection will eventually establish worlds of their own. The vision rhymes in certain ways with Octavia Butler's fictional Earthseed, a speculative, post-apocalyptic project that also involves space travel in the wake of social, economic, and environmental failure on Earth. Each proposes a frontier utopia that is imagined materially—the redoing of unresolved histories toward a potential future in which new worlds, in accordance with a new book of scripture, can finally be imagined and enacted, albeit toward different visions of a common good.

Poetry is redirected silence as well as redirected sound, a domain whereby the world is shaped for a time by the music of language, even when its meanings are beyond the reach of words.

If the received architectures of complicity and acquiescence come apart, what else might they become?

To disrupt the relationship of predator and prey, to reshape the relation between individual or collective agency and state power, is to renovate the lived and living world. No text, no history is immutable. The repeated unmaking and remaking of America—as a concept and as an ongoing textual project—is not impossible. It is happening all the time.

THE WORDS OF OTHERS ARE INSIDE ME

BEGIN ANYWHERE
John Cage and others.

THE END
See "Poetry, the True Fiction" by Barbara Guest in *Forces of Imagination: Writing on Writing* (2002).

SHE WHO WROTE
See the catalog by Sidney Babcock and Erhan Tamur, *She Who Wrote: Enheduanna and the Women of Mesopotamia, ca. 3400–2000 B.C* (2022), and Sophus Helle, *Enheduana: The Complete Poems of the World's First Author* (2023).

O PIONEER
Oxford English Dictionary.

Public Records of the Colony of Connecticut 1636–1776 (1850–1890).

Francis Bacon, *Of the Proficience and Advancement of Learning, Divine and Human* (1605).

Concerning agriculture, see Roxanne Dunbar-Ortiz, *An Indigenous Peoples' History of the United States* (2014).

James Hutton presented his "Theory (Concerning the System of the Earth, Its Duration, and Stability)" in July of 1785. A full account of Hutton's theory, based on observations of geographical "unconformity," was published in 1788.

A REGION MAY BE DEFINED . . . BY ITS BARRIERS TO PERCEPTION.
Excerpted from Erving Goffman, *The Presentation of Self in Everyday Life* (1956).

A COIN IS A MAP TO A BEHEADING
See Jean-Michel Basquiat's painting *Charles the First* (1982).

LIONTAMING IN AMERICA
William Cody, born on the Mississippi edge of Iowa Territory, toured his show from 1886 to 1891, though other near-death encounters were per-

formed before and after under his aegis, including the Cody, Wyoming rodeo, which is still in operation.

THE CINEMA HAS ALWAYS BEEN INTERESTED IN GOD
André Bazin.

THE NEXT VOICE YOU HEAR (1950)
Dir. William A. Wellman.

JOE SMITH, AMERICAN (1942)
Dir. Richard Thorpe.

THE PERILS OF PAULINE (1914)
Dir. Cecil B. DeMille.

THE BURNED-OVER DISTRICT
See Whitney R. Cross, *The Burned-over District* (1950); William R. Farrell, *Classical Place Names in New York State* (2002); William M. Beauchamp, *Aboriginal Place Names of New York* (1907).

FATHER, I AM BURNING
See Sigmund Freud, *Interpretation of Dreams* (1899).

INTERPRETATION OF DREAMS
Much of the language in this section has been extracted from Lucy Mack Smith's *Biographical Sketches of Joseph Smith, the Prophet, and His Progenitors for Many Generations* (1844).

AND THEN THERE HE WAS, AS IF EVERYBODY KNEW HIS NAME
See Gertrude Stein, *Four in America* (1947).

MR. QUINCY & MR. ADAMS
See "Joseph Smith at Nauvoo" by Josiah Quincy in *Figures of the Past* (1883).

[*sic*]
Passage from Patty Bartlett Sessions's diary, including diacritical marks, excerpted from *Mormon Midwife: The 1846–1888 Diaries of Patty Bartlett Sessions* (ed. Donna Toland Smart, 1999).

MRS. JACOBS & MRS. SMITH
Interview excerpted from *The Saints Herald* (January 11, 1905).

NEVER SAY HIGHER OR LOWER
From Charles Darwin's marginalia on Robert Chambers, *Vestiges of the Natural History of Creation* (1844).

TWIN EVILS OR EVIL TWINS
Margaret Rossiter coined the term "the Matilda effect" after Matilda Joslyn Gage.

MISS MANNING & MRS. JAMES
See Jane Elizabeth Manning James, *The Autobiography of Jane Elizabeth Manning James* (transcribed by Elizabeth J. D. Roundy, ca. 1902) and Quincy D. Newell, *Your Sister in the Gospel: The life of Jane Manning James, a Nineteenth-Century Black Mormon* (2019).

PERRIGRINE'S DREAM
Extracted from *Exemplary Elder: The Life and Missionary Diaries of Perrigrine Sessions, 1814–1893* (ed. Donna Toland Smart, 2002).

TYPES OF SECRETS
Excerpted from Erving Goffman's *The Presentation of Self in Everyday Life* (1956).

COIN OF THE REALM
See Sir Richard Francis Burton, *The City of the Saints* (1861).

MISS ADAMS & MRS. COBB
Passages extracted from correspondence held in the Theodore Schroeder papers, ca. 1846–1945, Manuscript and Archives Division at the New York Public Library.

MAUDE ADAMS AS SAINT JOAN (1909)
See Alphonse Marie Mucha's *Maude Adams as Joan of Arc*.

IF A LION SPOKE
Ludwig Wittgenstein.

BECAUSE IT IS ABSURD
Credo quia absurdum, widely attributed to Tertullian, is an Enlightenment-era misappropriation.

THE CIRCUS
Antony D. Hippisley Coxe, "The History of the Circus" (1956).

POLLY OF THE CIRCUS (1917)
Dirs. Charles T. Horan and Edwin L. Hollywood.

POLLY OF THE CIRCUS (1932)
Dir. Alfred Santell.

MR. ROBERTS
See *The Autobiography of B. H. Roberts* (ed. Gary J. Bergera, 1990) and Charles Dickens's essay "Bound for the Great Salt Lake" (1863).

ADVISE AND CONSENT (1962)
Dir. Otto Preminger.

THAT SOUND BELONGS TO A TIME THAT IS GONE
Violet in *The Great Lie* (1941), dir. Edmund Goulding.

CLOSE ENCOUNTERS (1977)
Close Encounters of the Third Kind, dir. Steven Spielberg.

FUTURE IMPERFECT
Angel of dust: See Nathaniel Mackey's ongoing epistolary novel *From a Broken Bottle Traces of Perfume Still Emanate.*

UNFINISHED RAMP
Robert Smithson died in a plane crash on July 20, 1973 while surveying the site of his last earthwork, *Amarillo Ramp*, while it was in process.

MOOD INDIGO
Broca's Paradox: "To see a blue light, you must not look directly at it," as recounted in Julia Kristeva's essay "Giotto's Joy" (1982).

Flood: Quotation slip for the *Oxford English Dictionary*. (Photograph by Daphne Preston-Kendal. Courtesy of Wikimedia).

Film still fragment from *Lost in Space* unaired pilot (CBS Broadcasting, 1965).

The Greatest Natural & National Curiosity in the World: Fragment of Joice Heth exhibition promotional handbill created by J. Booth & Son, ca. 1835 (Used by permission, Somers Historical Society).

McConnell, James. *Historical Maps of the United States*. Chicago, Ill.: McConnell Map Co., 1919 (Courtesy of the McConnell Map Collection, Library of Congress). Stitching by the author.

Grant Wood, *Parson Weems' Fable* (1939), oil on canvas, 38 3/8 x 50 1/8 in.: painting fragment (Courtesy of the Amon Carter Museum of American Art, Fort Worth, Texas, 1970.43).

Sitting Bull and Buffalo Bill, Montreal, Quebec, 1885: Photograph fragment (Courtesy of the McCord Stewart Museum).

Recording MGM lion roar (Unknown source, 1928).

Excerpt from "Gen. Smith's Views on the Government and Policy of the U.S." (*Times and Seasons*, Nauvoo, Ill. May 15, 1844). White-out redactions by the author.

Eliza Snow in Cairo, 1873 (Used by permission of the Utah State Historical Society).

Film still fragment from *House of Frankenstein* (dir. Erle C. Fenton, Universal Pictures, 1944).

Tintype of two women (Collection of the author).

Brigham Young and unidentified woman (Courtesy of the Church History Library, The Church of Jesus Christ of Latter-day Saints, PH7848).

Perrigrine Sessions (Courtesy of Suzanne Brown Anderson).

Lucina Call, Fanny Emmorett Loveland, Sarah Crossley, and Sarah Ann Bryson (seated) with Esther Mabey, Perrigrine Sessions (cut off), and Elizabeth Bridno (standing) in the entry to the Sessions Tavern (Courtesy of Suzanne Brown Anderson).

Maude Adams as a child (Used by permission of the Utah State Historical Society).

Salt Lake City Theatre interior (Courtesy of the Church History Library, The Church of Jesus Christ of Latter-day Saints, PH 1603).

Maude Adams as Joan of Arc, ca. 1909 (Photograph by Charles Frohman from J. Willis Sayre Collection of Theatrical Photographs. Courtesy of Wikimedia).

Maude Adams and her mother Annie Adams Kiskadden, May 10, 1902 (Used by permission of the Utah State Historical Society).

Dosso Dossi, *Circe and Her Lovers in a Landscape* (ca. 1525), oil on canvas, 39 11/16 x 53 9/16 in.: Painting fragment (Courtesy of the National Gallery of Art, Washington DC).

Hyrum Bischoff, Book of Mormon lecture (Collection of the author).

Utah State Prison from Northwest, 1903 (Used by permission of the Utah State Historical Society).

Film still fragment from *Close Encounters of the Third Kind* (Dir. Steven Spielberg, Columbia Pictures, 1977).

Overhead view of Bingham Canyon Mine, Utah (Used by permission of Universal Images Group North America LLC / DeAgostini / Alamy Stock Photo).

Exit to Plymouth (Photograph by Tom Valazak of CrossCountryRoads. com, used with permission).

ACKNOWLEDGMENTS

My thanks to all those who have accompanied me during the making of this book.

Belated thanks to my parents, Ronald Porter Willis and Thora Belle Brown Willis.

My thanks to Suzanne Brown Anderson and her late husband Lou who provided a wealth of information and direction through decades of inquiry. Thanks to Robert Willis for his kind and clearheaded memories of his childhood with my father. Thanks to the late Loretta Bischoff for sharing her father's archive and to Elsie Martens for opening her home to me.

I am indebted to my siblings and especially grateful to my sister Patty for years of conversation about the meanings of community, especially among women.

I would not be here without the shared imagination and love of my family of affinity. You know who you are—in, among, and beyond these lines. My thanks to Myung Mi Kim, Lisa Jarnot, and Julia Conrad for their comments on this text, and to Nancy Kuhl for wisdom and expertise at the intersection of archives and family. My thanks to Simone White and to W. Paul Reeve for their notes on passages that appear in these pages. A special thanks to Lisa Cohen, whose comments on this work over many years—and whose own writing about relation—have been as crucial and instructive to me as her practice of friendship.

Thanks to the editors of *Harper's Magazine*, *The New York Review of Books*, and *Poetry* for publishing poems included here. Thanks to *e-flux* for publishing an earlier version of "Future Imperfect." Thanks to the editors at *The New Yorker* and *Evening Will Come* for publishing texts related to and overlapping with this work. Thanks to Khushal Gujadhur for assistance with the images in this book.

To Michael Flaum, beloved collaborator in the ongoing evolution of home and belonging: Hello again. My thanks for things that only you can name.

I am grateful for the support of the Guggenheim Foundation, Lannan Foundation, Ucross Foundation, Hobart and William Smith Colleges' Trias Residency, and the University of Iowa.

My thanks to Terrell Butler, who brought me into conversation with Augustine's *Confessions* in my year at Mr. Young's university. I hope this message finds you.

Thanks to many other passionate keepers of intersecting histories: to Ken Fox at the George Eastman House Museum, to Liz Rogers and Rachel Ernst at the J. Willard Marriott Library Special Collections at the University of Utah, to Karen Spragg at the Lovell-Kane Area Museum, to Greg Walz at the Utah Historical Society, to Jeff Thompson and Jay Burrup at the LDS Church Archives, and to the archivists in the Manuscripts Division at the New York Public Library who oversee the Theodore Schroeder Archive.

Thanks beyond measure to Jeffrey Yang at New Directions for crucial feedback, trust, and patience—and for believing in this work over the years as it wrestled its way into being.

ELIZABETH WILLIS is the author of eight books of poetry, including *Alive: New and Selected Poems*, a finalist for the Pulitzer Prize. She teaches at the Iowa Writers' Workshop.